grief

SPEAK

VOLUME 1

Stories of Loss

DR. MARI NARDOLILLO-DIAS

Grief Speak: Stories of Loss, volume 1.
Copyright © 2021 Dr. Mari Nardolillo-Dias.
Produced and printed
by Stillwater River Publications.
All rights reserved. Written and produced in the
United States of America.
This book may not be reproduced
or sold in any form without the expressed, written
permission of the author and publisher.
Visit our website at
www.StillwaterPress.com
for more information.
First Stillwater River Publications Edition
Library of Congress Control Number: 2021903622
Paperback ISBN: 978-1-952521-82-9
Hardcover ISBN: 978-1-952521-91-1
1 2 3 4 5 6 7 8 9 10
Written by Dr. Mari Nardolillo-Dias
Cover design inspired by Pati Paolella.
Published by Stillwater River Publications,
Pawtucket, RI, USA.
Publisher's Cataloging-In-Publication Data
(Prepared by The Donohue Group, Inc.)

Names: Nardolillo-Dias, Mari, author.
Title: Grief speak. Volume 1, Stories of loss / Dr. Mari
Nardolillo-Dias.
Other Titles: Griefspeak | Stories of loss
Description: First Stillwater River Publications edition. |
Pawtucket, RI, USA : Stillwater River Publications, [2021]
| A collection of columns on grief published online and in
blogs.
Identifiers: ISBN 9781952521829 (paperback) | ISBN
9781952521911 (hardcover)
Subjects: LCSH: Grief. | Loss (Psychology) | Psychic
trauma. | Epidemics--Psychological aspects. | Death--Psy-
chological aspects.
Classification: LCC BF575.G7 N369 2021 | DDC
155.937--dc23

This book is dedicated to
all the grievers, past, present and future

To my Absolute
fitures fellow
members.

Be well

— Maci

"We do not tell stories as they are,
we tell stories as we are"

~Anais Nin

Blue

I'm not here to preach, cause I'm right there with you
No judgment to pass just helping you through
No one can tell you how long it should take
Some heal quickly, some crushed by the weight

So, don't feel rushed no one knows but you
What it takes till you're no longer blue

(There's no) timeline for healing - For pain you are feeling
No matter the time that's gone by
No timeline for healing - For nights you are reeling
You know it's ok to still cry
I'll be blue for you, I'll be blue for you

The tears and the heartache, the mess of it all
Picking yourself back up after you fall
Only to lose faith and fall once again
Does not mean you're weak, it's a place we've all been

So, don't feel rushed no one knows but you
What it takes till you're no longer blue

(There's no) timeline for healing - For pain you are feeling
No matter the time that's gone by
No timeline for healing - For nights you are reeling
You know it's ok to still cry
I'll be blue for you, I'll be blue for you

So, do what is right for you, do what you need to do
Do all the things that will bring back the joy to you
I'll be blue for you, I'll be blue for you

(There's no) timeline for healing - For pain you are feeling
No matter the time that's gone by
No timeline for healing - For nights you are reeling
You know it's ok to still cry
I'll be blue for you, I'll be blue for you

(lyrics reprinted with permission. Joe Matira and Dean
Petrella, April 2020)

Table of Contents

PART 1 - LOSS OF A LOVED ONE

PART 2 - DEALING WITH A PANDEMIC

Foreword

I "met" Mari Dias through her writing. I was representing an author who wrote about the suicide of her adult son. I connected the two because there was a soul-sharing that was obvious and that I knew so little about. Mari had a radio show at the time and my client would go on and talk about her own book, and I would listen to see that the speaking points were hit, and nothing left out or needing to be clarified. And I was drawn into her own story.

As a writer, and an educator, and a therapist, she touched each one of those audiences in a unique way. Her ability to communicate with passion, with understanding, and with the willingness to share her own journey is unusual. What is even more unusual is to be moved so much by a story of serious loss when you may have not experienced such loss yourself. Yet the story has meaning for the life you are living - and the loss you know will be in your own future - one day to come.

Today, Mari writes for my digital news site, RINewsToday. Each Friday a new work is featured. I can tell by looking at the numbers on the back end of the site, how many people relate to Mari. As in a personal relationship she has felt more comfortable with the audience, so she shares a bit more over time.

We learn that she is The Mortician's Daughter. And how deeply this touches us. in so many ways. As a feminist living a new time, but growing up in an older, more traditional one. Growing up playing around the business of caskets and being quiet as mourners shared the large building that was also her home. And then there is this:

> "When I die there will be no questions to ask. Why? Because I'm in the business of death and dying and this is what you think about. You plan. I've worked with too many clients who deal with unanswered questions. I've been planning my exit for years, having prearranged my wake, funeral and burial. Just to make sure it's done right. My way. I've been doing this for over 15 years. My obituary is written in the first person and completed, except for the date of death, and updated, along with my resume, on a regular basis. It begins with my favorite Mary Oliver quote: "Tell me what you plan to do with your one wild and precious life?"

Her simple yet ever so complex writing has not left me pondering my own death. But it has left me asking myself this, *""Tell me what you plan to do with your one wild and precious life?"*.

Her words will not rest easy, but they will nudge you a little bit. They will come back to you at a wake, or funeral of a stranger. But when it is your time to grieve closer, they will wrap themselves around you with great meaning - and leave you with a sense of the circle of life - and the hope we must have to live in it with acceptance and peace.

Nancy Thomas
Publisher, RINewsToday
Owner, Tapestry Communications

Introduction

"What's the matter with me?" How many times have you asked yourself this question? How many times has someone asked you that same question? What's the matter with you?"

When you ask yourself that question, follow up with another. "What have I lost? If you have lost something, I suspect you are grieving. We grieve for any loss, whether due to death (finite) or non-death (non-finite loss). I believe that given the pandemic, several of you are grieving a non-death loss and perhaps a death loss as well. Loss of independence, a relationship, a job, or loss of mental stability.

The pandemic has increased our losses exponentially. We have lost our "normal," our independence, our ability to physically touch someone. To see someone's smile. How do you deal with this grief? The numbness, anxiety, sadness, and depression are not just the purview of a bereaved person at a funeral or memorial. It is a host of thoughts and feelings that affect us in the most unusual ways. There is even something called "physical grief," where the pain and sadness manifest themselves in head and stomach aches, and even heart aches. Because we have experienced a loss.

Now that you know you may be grieving, what should you do? This book is a compilation of stories, many that include thoughts on solutions, told by real people during the most vulnerable and difficult time of their lives. Some of these stories focus on end- of- life experiences, others on life after death. Or life before life. Still others explore experiences with the non-death losses associated with the pandemic. We have lost a great deal of personal freedom. And we grieve for what once was.

This book also includes many stories about death and loss as well. A thwarted suicide, a young dad's heart attack, an old woman who (almost) dies alone. There is no need to read the stories in order. Remember that these are personal stories, told in the safety of my grief therapy office. We are all fortunate that these individuals agreed to share their experiences.

I am a grief therapist. A death doula. A mortician's daughter. I have dedicated much of my life to working with loss. Trust me. There is a story just waiting for you to read. Its impact will be immeasurable.

-Mari

grief
SPEAK

Part 1

Loss of a Loved One

THIRTEEN STORIES

Good Grief?

As a practicing thanatologist the most frequently asked question I receive is, "Am I grieving correctly?"

"I can't sleep."

"I'm having severe gastrointestinal issues."

"My neck is stiff and I can't move it."

"I can't stop crying." "I am having migraines." "I can't get out of bed."

"I'm angry at everyone."

"My child died a year ago and people are telling me to move on. Am I grieving too long?"

"Is there something wrong with me?" "Am I crazy?"

The short answer is yes. And no, you are not crazy. Grief often affects sleep and eating habits, causes incessant tears and what I refer to as "bathrobe days" — those days when you have no interest or energy to get dressed or speak with anyone, and all you want to do is lie in bed. Moreover, there is no timetable for grief, although the type of death we experience can affect our grieving practices. A sudden, traumatic death of a young person may exacerbate the length and severity of the grieving process.

Each of the quotes above are indicative of typical responses to grief. Not everyone experiences physical grief, but many do. Physical grief occurs when your sadness and pain manifests itself in your body. This often occurs because the experience of grief wreaks havoc on our immune systems and creates a perfect storm of physical ailments. Before you run to see your primary doctor or a specialist, get in touch with your grief.

Grief is like a mountain and so many try to climb over or go around the mountain in order to avoid the pain. Others numb themselves with alcohol, food, work, or drugs. Some project their anger and hurt onto others in order to externalize their grief. We need to go through the mountain and feel our heart break. It begins as *acute grief*, much like acute appendicitis. We experience constant, severe pain, sometimes causing us to double over, and we rush for medication or an emergency room. Acute conditions are temporary. At some point (and it is different for everyone), our acute grief morphs into *chronic grief*. Much like a chronic medical condition, it is ongoing and vacillates. You have both good and bad hours or days, where one day the pain is unbearable and the next manageable. On another note, there is *complicated grief*, where we experience acute symptoms long after the death without the transition to chronic grief. Diagnosed complicated grief requires a specialized therapeutic approach.

According to Henry Wadsworth Longfellow, "There is no grief like the grief that does not speak." This statement provides us with direction as to how to get through the mountain. GriefSpeak. Talk about your grief. Join a support group through your church or synagogue or local hospice organization, or search social media where ubiquitous grief chat rooms are plentiful. There are others grieving at two o'clock in the morning — you are not alone. Finally, meeting with a grief therapist is not a sign of weakness or mental illness.

Grief manifests itself in physical, psychological, emotional, neurological, and behavioral ways. Give yourself permission to experience profound loss and speak your grief.

Life after Life

"She said, she said I know what it's like to be dead"
(The Beatles, "She Said, She Said," 1966)

The year 2020 has been difficult for many, and devasting for some. Despite all things COVID, quarantine, and the state of the nation, life and death go on. There is no hiatus or sabbatical on the journey of life. Childbirths go on, as do child deaths. Births garner excitement and hopefulness for the future. Children's deaths stop our collective breaths and the beats of our hearts. Sometimes we are soothed with a timid solace that there is life after death. Life after life.

Belief in some kind of afterlife often comforts the grieving. Do you believe in a higher power? Is there a heaven? Do we go back into the earth and feed trees and flowers? Perhaps we reincarnate and come back in the soul of a newborn? Existentialists believe life is the end of any type of existence. We didn't exist before we were born, and we will cease to exist upon death.

Some often use the term "old soul" when referring to a young person. According to the urban dictionary, an old soul can simply refer to "someone who is wise beyond their years, more understanding of the world around them." However, an alternate meaning includes "a person who has learned from past incarnations, or lives."

I am currently working with several families whose children have died. Each family has referred to their child as an "old soul." One family came to accept the death of a toddler, stating that "I knew from the day they were born that they weren't meant to be on earth very long. They would make their mark and leave us too early. Too early for us, yet the right time for them."

Another family grieving the sudden death of a child describes a young, short life so replete with happiness, success, and the thrill of living that may rival a long, long life of an elderly person who identifies with John Mellencamp's lyrics, "Life goes on, long after the thrill of living is gone." (1982, "Jack and Diane")

The death of a child, and particularly if sudden and/or unexplained, is a traumatic death, and with trauma can come a grief that "weighs you down like your own flesh, only more of it, an obesity of grief" (Ellen Bass). We try to make meaning out of the death of children.

"The loss of a child is not one finite event. It is a continuous loss that unfolds minute by minute over the course of a lifetime. This is why grief lasts forever. This ripple effect lasts forever. The bleeding never stops… Empty spaces, that should be full, everywhere we go. There is and will always be a missing space in our lives. Time does not make the space less empty…I now take nothing for granted, but I am grateful beyond words. I have my son to thank for that. Being his mom is the best gift I've ever been given. Even death can't take that away" (Angela Miller, *A Bed for my Heart*).

There exist mounds of both anecdotal and empirical attempts at evidence of life after life. Those like Scarlett Lewis hold tightly onto the belief that her son, Jesse, the youngest victim of the Sandy Hook Massacre, is everywhere. She maintains a strong connection with him as signs appear on a daily basis, confirming her beliefs (Lewis, 2013, *Nurturing Healing Love*). For those who hunger for a more scientific approach, Eben Alexander, a prominent neurosurgeon, writes of his near-death experience in *Proof of Heaven*. Despite his background in the science of the mind, Alexander insists he journeyed beyond this world.

In his groundbreaking book, Raymond Moody investigates near-death experiences and points out that these experiences have been reported in human beings for thousands of years. Moody includes thousands of subjects and conducted a qualitative study and searched for a thematic code. The similarities in subjects' experiences leave little doubt about the perceived veracity of these experiences. (*Life After Life*, 1975)

In my own professional practice, I spend a great deal of time "holding space" at death beds. I often hear the dying speak as if they were between two worlds – one in reality and the other in a netherworld. They often speak to deceased relatives and friends, assuring them that:

"I'm coming! Have some patience. I have to wait for the Super Bowl party."

Yet, the belief of life after life sometimes "soothes the savage soul." I remember hearing a story about a grieving father at the gravesite of his 16-year-old daughter. The priest, seeing that the man was weeping uncontrollably, asked him a powerful question:

"If, on the day of her birth, God said, 'You may have this beautiful, loving, talented daughter; however, I will have to take her back in 16 years. Do you still want her?'" I believe for those who believe in a higher power, your response would be a resounding yes!

Some have answered the conundrum "life after life" for us. Dr. Mary Neal, following her drowning in a kayak accident, reveals her terror as she was pinned at the bottom of the rapids, completely submerged. Despite the rescue efforts, she was underwater too long, and as a result, died. When asked "What's it like to be dead," she replied, "I know what it's like to be dead. There is life after life. It was a seamless, peaceful, and beautiful [experience]. I felt quite wonderful." (*To Heaven and Back*). Neal's description of life after life (if believed), may provide an uncomfortable ease to grieving parents whose children's lives ended unfinished. We grieve for ourselves and the remainder of the unfinished life. Yet, death ends a life, not a relationship.

She's Come Undone

She's come undone
She didn't know what she was headed for
And when [she] found what she was headed for
It was too late.
She's come undone."
(The Guess Who, "Undun," 1969)

It's September 2020. Monica's nativity scene remains on display. Her suitcase from a trip in February sits, unpacked. When she opens the refrigerator, she recognizes a once-fresh chocolate cream pie, now gone bad, along with a watermelon and an assortment of Dave's Market containers whose contents are unidentifiable.

I should empty this fridge and just leave a box of Arm & Hammer and some batteries, she thinks. She closed the refrigerator and poured herself a glass of suspect orange juice, still sitting on the counter. Laundry remains unwashed.

8

Her husband, Evan, worries that his once-dynamic wife is coming undone. He returns home from work every afternoon to find her binge-watching "Call the Midwife" on Netflix. She tells him it's her calm. Evan feels helpless. Then he feels hopeful. He offers a respite:

"Let's rent a camper and take the kids up north for a long weekend." Monica nods without voice as she continues to watch poor women in London go through labor and delivery. She never lifts her head or makes eye contact. She is still dressed in her quarantine clothes – sweats that she wears to bed and does not change as the next day dawns. She wears a baseball cap, which disguises her unwashed hair.

Monica's lukewarm response to Evan's suggestion was just enough for him to pursue his plan. He rented a decent camper with enough room for all five of them. Evan and Monica have 3 children, all under the age of 10, each required to complete their remote schoolwork daily. Monica can't help them. She can't help herself.

Evan took responsibility for packing the camper. He found dozens of cans of Campbell's chicken and rice soup hidden in the back of the kitchen pantry. They would be a quick and easy lunch for the kids, he thought. He packed the cans in a canvas carry-on and added them to his newly purchased groceries.

Monica brought along a brown paper bag that contained red licorice, a bathrobe, and her medications, which were anti-anxiety and antidepressants, whose prescriptions had been increased exponentially since the pandemic. Evan took care to help the children pack. They were excited. They could accomplish their schoolwork on vacation.

Once they were all packed, gassed up, and ready to go, Monica suddenly stopped in her tracks and demanded that they bring a car along.

"I don't want to be stuck in a trailer park. We can't travel on short trips with this monstrosity. We need to bring the car along as well."

Evan didn't like the idea. He knew Monica would need to drive the car as he didn't think she could maneuver the camper.

"Monica, honey, I don't think that's a good idea. You haven't driven for months. Since the beginning of the pandemic."

"Evan, DO NOT treat me like a child. I'll drive the car and follow right behind you." She could not be dissuaded. The children wanted to ride in the camper, but her youngest, Antoinette, didn't want her mom to drive alone.

"I'll keep Mom company in the car," she said in her mature five-year-old voice. "I don't mind."

Evan didn't want this trip to begin with an argument. He also felt a bit optimistic that Monica, for the first time since the quarantine, displayed some of her old "fire."

"Alright, Monica. You follow us closely and we will take a few breaks along the way. Antoinette, you can ride with Mom, but behave and don't distract her while she's driving. Monica, you and I will communicate through our cell phones. We both have Bluetooth."

Monica seemed pleased. They got into their respective vehicles, with her two boys waving from the camper to Monica and Antoinette in the car. They headed north. Monica didn't know what she was headed for, as Evan had planned a surprise destination. Monica hated surprises.

It was a lovely Friday morning, the beginning of a long holiday weekend. It was early, so traffic was light. Evan remained diligent, checking his rear-view mirror. He began to relax. Monica was directly behind him. He checked his-side view mirrors, ignoring the warning that "objects may be closer than they appear."

Deep into New Hampshire, both vehicles entered the scenic Kancamagus highway. The boys were taking pictures of the scenery with Evan's iPhone. Monica blasted her radio, where she had "Bye, bye, Miss American Pie" on repeat on Spotify. Antoinette had heard it so often along the way that she joined in and sang with her mom.

The Kancamagus can be a roller coaster, with sharp inclines, declines, and turns.

"And them good ole boys were drinking whiskey and rye," could be heard blasting out the open windows. Monica was craving fresh, clean air. As they headed down a sharp decline, Monica noticed the brake lights on the camper, and knew Evan was riding his brakes to slow down. She did the same; however, her brakes didn't work. She began to pick up speed and, in an effort to avoid hitting the camper, she swerved and passed them on the left. Evan watched what was happening. He tried calling Monica's cell phone. It went directly to voice mail.

Monica and Antoinette were now careening down the decline, far ahead of the camper.

Evan thought quickly. He accelerated in the hopes of catching up to the car. Irrationally, he thought that he could be of help if he were in closer proximity.

He thought, *does she remember or have the capacity to think about alternative ways to stop the car.* He continued to call and leave voice mail: "Monica, throw it in park. Pull up the parking brake. You need to stop the car!" More than six voice mails. Evan continued to accelerate. He could see the car in the distance. He drove faster. Eighty miles per hour.

The decline seemed to level out. Evan reassured himself that the car would come to a stop. It didn't. Evan saw the accident long before he arrived at the scene. Monica had swerved left to avoid the cars in her lane and hit a car head-on coming up from the opposite lane, its passengers returning from their vacation.

Evan called 911 but arrived on the scene before they did. The music was still blasting on Spotify. Both Monica and Antoinette were thrown from the car, landing on a "photo spot," the best view of the mountains. They were both dead, lying in a comforting position, almost entwined, yet giving them the best view of the mountains. They both had smiles on their faces.

Evan screamed. Then he saw the other car. There was an elderly couple, still in their seats with seat belts fastened, their Dunkin' Donut coffees still hot and sitting in the cup holders. Rescues, fire, and police arrived.

Evan had told the boys to stay in the camper. However, when they saw the lights and heard the sirens, they jumped out of the camper and ran across the street, unaware of additional rescue vehicles approaching the scene.

Evan wasn't looking back. He was looking down. At his wife and daughter, tourists in New Hampshire who never made it to the surprise destination. Evan jumped, startled when he heard a second screech of tires, this time coming from a rescue vehicle. The driver didn't see the boys. Both boys died instantly on impact.

Evan was numb. He lost his ability to breathe. Rescue workers approached him with a blanket and oxygen. He was so still he resembled a statue cut out of the granite scenery.

The rescue took the bodies away. Evan remained frozen. The music was still playing in the car. Over and over. "Bye, bye, Miss American Pie…and good ole boys were drinking whiskey and rye, singin' this'll be the day that I die." (Don McLean)

Without thinking, Evan began to move. To walk. He walked off to the side of the Kancamagus, passing by the spot where his wife and daughter had recently been.

It was a beautiful Friday afternoon, the beginning of a long holiday weekend. Traffic was light. But enough for a disaster.

Evan walked parallel to the highway, walking aimlessly, without direction. He followed a tourist trail. One foot in front of the other. He smelled the pines, felt the sun, and the altitude affected his breathing.

As he walked, he thought, *"Why Breathe Alone?"**

*(Dean Petrella, lead singer and lyricist for The Complaints, from "Another Lover," unpublished)

The Loss of Older Loved Ones

"And wherever you've gone
And wherever we might go
It don't seem fair… today just disappeared
Your light's reflected now, reflected from afar
We were but stones, your light made us stars"
("Light Years," lyrics by Eddie Vedder)

I attended two memorials this week. Both mothers and grand-mothers, one a national treasure and the other a local one. One was that of the notorious RBG, Judge Ruth Bader Ginsburg, the second that of Auntie Dee. Both women lived long and productive lives, both full of light, and then both disappeared. It is the longevity of their lives, and the traditional response to an older person's death that struck me. RBG at 87, Auntie Dee at 94.

Despite her long life and several battles with cancer, RBG extended her life by "nothing short of miracles." She was Jewish, born of immigrants (her father from Odessa). She was an icon. She was quoted at her televised memorial by Chief Justice

Roberts: "I wanted to be an opera singer when I was younger." He added, "Instead, she was a rock star."

There is no ignoring the thud of RBG's words, her persona, and her confidence. A tiny woman with a soft voice, whose words spoke loudly in the halls of the Supreme Court. Thousands are mourning her death. Thousands who never knew her. They didn't have to. Her reputation and impact on women's rights are legendary, and her death marks the end of an era in her history, as well as ours. She is described as tough, brave, a fighter. Her memorial was conducted by a rabbi and readings from the Torah were read in Hebrew.

Auntie Dee was born of Italian immigrants, the last remaining of 9 children, symbolizing the end of a generation. We are the next. Also a tiny woman with a rather loud voice, she was described as tough, brave, and a fighter as well. There was a thud to Auntie Dee's words. Her home was the Italian hub for her siblings and extended family. Holidays were special with Dee at the helm. Multiple courses of homemade delicacies, including the traditional *la Vigilia* (feast of the seven fishes) on Christmas Eve. She was a quintessential hostess, a gregarious, outspoken lover of life and the beach. Unlike RBG, Auntie Dee was not a national hero, or a maker of history, but to her family, she was. Her memorial was conducted by a priest, and readings from the Bible were read in English.

We in this world are not so different from each other. We may have different rituals and traditions in death, but these traditions and rituals connect us with our ancestors, our families, and our culture. In fact, we are more similar to each other than we think. Every culture has their way of saying goodbye.

Yet in our American culture, we tend to negate the grief displayed for an older person. When you tell others that your elderly loved one died, they often ask, "How old were they?" It seems to make a difference to them. It may determine their level of understanding and empathy for your sadness.

When we respond with an advanced number, the usual retort is, "Oh. Well, he/she lived a long life. You're lucky to have had them that long."

No, we are not lucky. It is never long enough.

Clients tell me that they feel apologetic for grieving so strongly and long as few people seem to get it. They suggest that they sometimes hide their tears, feeling guilty. As one angry client, Felicia argued with the air:

"Don't you dare deny me my grief! My mother held a space in me, and I am grieving for myself. She will no longer be there to share a cup of coffee, a phone call, or just to hear her voice. Just the knowing that I can't is what overwhelms me. She has been beside me since I was born. She is part of me."

When we mourn an older loved one, the tears flow just as freely, the heartache still shears the depth of our pain. Most people will not understand. It is expected at an advanced age. Yet expectations, or anticipatory grief, does not lighten the pain of their death.

We celebrate their lives, mourn them in death. We are never prepared to lose a loved one, despite their advanced age. I expect that Judge Ruth Bader Ginsburg's family is sad and grieving, as is Auntie Dee's family.

It's never easy to let go. It's never easy to move on. We can love them through their aging, their wrinkled faces, their forgetfulness, arthritic hands, and stooped posture. We've never known life without them.

We take care of them as they once took care of us.

And we cry the desperate tears of loss. Don't let anyone tell you otherwise.

Mother's Day for Motherless Children

Mother's Day is upon us, a day filled with celebration or grief. It was 1927 when Blind Willie Johnson recorded the song "Motherless Children," which was made popular by many, including Bob Dylan, Steven Miller, and Eric Clapton. The lyrics recognize that all children are impacted by the death of their mother.

Fast forward to 1997, when Hope Edelman published her groundbreaking book *Motherless Daughters*, which emphasizes the unique relationship between daughters and mothers – "a daughter's life is irrevocably altered; that this one fact forever changes who she is and who she will be. Gone is the caregiver, teacher, adversary, role model, and guide to being a woman."

Rhode Island's own Ann Hood recently published an essay in AGNI, a literary magazine, entitled "Stop Breath" about her relationship with and the death of her mom Gloria, affectionately known as Gogo. This essay, rife with losses, provides a poignant, personal insight into a mother/daughter relationship. The loss of Gogo feels like the loss of every woman's mother as the reader grieves not only for Gogo, but for their own mom. Yet reading Hood's essay encourages the reader to remember the small things, the intimate, everyday details of our lives with Mom.

Research tends to focus on the relationship between mothers and daughters primarily during childhood, as it is a crucial stage of development. In addition, same gender parents seem to have the biggest impact on children. In 1991 Virginia Apperson, a Jungian analyst wrote an article entitled "Motherless Children" revisiting the impact of the loss on all children, as did the lyrics of 1927.

To all motherless children of all ages: As you place flowers on the gravesite of your mom, remember the small things. Remember her smell, the sound of her laugh, her quirky phrases, and the taste of her cooking. And for those who recently became motherless during this pandemic, I share your pain and wish I could hold it in the palm of my hand to lighten the weight of your grief, if only for a short time. Grief is like a mountain. Some may attempt to go around it, some to climb over it; however, as painful as it is, we must learn to go through it, burrowing a tunnel as we struggle to breathe. We will find ways to come out the other side, and eventually remember her smell, the sound of her laugh, her quirky phrases, and the taste of her cooking.

Everyone Has a Backstory

The caller opened our phone conversation with a question:

"Are abortions considered elective surgery during this pandemic?" she asked. I didn't know the answer but even if I did, I would not have simply provided a response. I knew there was a backstory. Everyone has a story.

She identified herself as Eve, and when asked, I explored the backstory. In my mind I am thinking, *why would she contact me, a grief center, rather than Planned Parenthood or the state?* It's always what the clients do not say that's telling.

Following a few prompts, Eve explained that she is in her mid-forties, unhappily married with children, and met a young man who had "stolen her heart and soul." "I would have divorced and married him, baby or no baby."

Eve defended her actions before she shared exactly what had happened. "Let's call him Adam," she said. Adam was considerably younger than Eve but the age, according to her, was not a detriment. "He is my soulmate," Eve offered through her

20

sobs. "We have so much in common! Our shared culture, our values and beliefs about death, our existential philosophy about life. We shared so much in a short time, including lovemaking. I loved him."

"Perhaps you still do," I responded.

"Well, my feelings for him play little role in my decision. (really?) As you probably figured out, I am pregnant with Adam's child. I know it is Adam's because I have not been intimate with my husband for months and months. Adam does not want the baby. He argued that he's too young and he doesn't want children. 'I'm just a kid!' he derided.

"Of course, me being married was another issue, but I am convinced that even if I were single, I would still be making this call. There are several things that make this even more gutwrenching. I love children and I am a staunch Catholic and prolife. This conundrum is killing me. How do I go against my strong beliefs and terminate this pregnancy without living with regret and pain? A baby that was, and then, wasn't. God would be very angry with me, and I with myself. Unlike many, I have a deep personal relationship with the truth. And the truth is this abortion is going to emotionally paralyze me for the rest of my life. If I choose to keep the baby, with a father who does not want it and a husband who will know it is not his, well, it's a no-win situation.

"I know, I know, I could step out of the truth and have sex with my husband so it would be feasible that it might be his. Or I could go away when I begin to show and then put the baby up for adoption. This is what goes through my mind twenty-four-seven. I thought I had made my decision as I dialed your number, but this virus may not offer me the option for abortion,

Loss of a Loved One

for killing a human being if the procedure is considered non-essential. If I must wait, it may be too late. The decision would be made for me. And I would consider myself a murderer for the rest of my life."

I responded with a comment she had not expressed. "Sounds like you are torn but, in your heart, you don't know if you can live with the decision to have an abortion. It also seems like you are considering the abortion for Adam, not for you. And he does not want the child, correct?"

She muffled a sob-filled "No. He does not."

"So, you are willing to go against all your religious beliefs and potentially be haunted by this for the rest of your life for him? Am I hearing you correctly?"

"Yes, I know I should do what is right for me and not Adam," said Eve. "But he is not in love with me. I thought he was. The connection seemed unbreakable. I thought we felt the same. The pregnancy showed me the objective truth that perhaps was there all along, but I did not want to see.

"I just cannot keep this baby, regardless of how badly I want it. Pretending it was my husband's is an option but, you know, I would be living an anxiety-ridden life, always trying to hide. I do not regret one minute with Adam, not even the pregnancy. I thought it would draw us even closer if that was possible. Adoption? Probably the best option but I know once I saw the baby, I would not be able to give it away. So yes, I have decided on the abortion and I will accept the lifelong consequences. Is it considered an elective procedure? Please, please, tell me no."

NOTE: Following careful research, the idea of abortions as elective procedures varies from state to state. Although West

Virginia, Ohio, Iowa, Alabama, Oklahoma, and Texas have put abortions on hold, other states have won lawsuits given this time-sensitive issue." PPSNE (Planned Parenthood of Southern New England), which include 17 centers in Connecticut and Rhode Island, remains open. Massachusetts has kept their Planned Parenthood open as well.

NOTE: Eve had her abortion, alone, in Massachusetts. It was a boy. She named him Christian James. Adam was at a baseball game.

Forever in my Heart

I Miss you

Valentine's Day for a Broken-Hearted Mom

"The hardest thing I've ever had to hear was that my child died.
The hardest thing I'll ever have to do
is to live every day since that moment."
(amourningmom.com)

There is no time limit on grief.

Today marks the 32nd Valentine's Day that Anna will go without hearts, flowers, or candy from her daughter Amanda. It was Christmas Eve, 1987 when Anna, excited for her first child, went into labor and delivered a beautiful, healthy, baby girl. She and her husband, David, chose the name "Amanda," a fitting moniker for the love they shared for their first and only daughter, as "Amanda" means "deserved to be loved." And indeed, she was. Christmas was extra special that year for the entire extended family.

As most families of Italian Catholic ancestry, Anna and David planned Amanda's baptism, replete with the white christening gown and the mandatory family and friends' festivities, with good homemade food and wine. Everyone present had an opportunity to kiss Amanda, imparting their own personal blessings as she was passed from the cradled arms of one to another. Anna looked on, feeling blessed with the joy of her daughter and the love everyone was pouring over her. It was a very special day.

Within a week of this christening, baby Amanda was dead. She was three months old. Anna noticed some discomfort on Amanda's part and brought her to the pediatrician, just to be on the safe side. The doctor put Amanda on Amoxicillin for an ear infection and Anna took her home. Anna administered the prescribed antibiotic and put Amanda to sleep for a well-deserved nap in Nona Paula's arms, thinking Amanda was just sleeping. A short time later, they began to question whether the baby was just asleep and panicked. They immediately called 911, which transported Amanda to the hospital, where she died on St. Joseph's Day, March 1988.

No, it was not SIDS (sudden infant death syndrome), and obviously not an ear infection. The autopsy revealed meningitis, a particularly virulent strain called meningococcal sepsis. Evidently the pediatrician did check the telling red mark on the back of Amanda's neck, usually one of the first indications of meningitis. Amanda did have the mark, but the doctor dismissed it, stating that "several dark-haired babies have that particular mark without indication of meningitis."

According to Anna, "Everybody and their mother (literally) held and kissed Amanda at the christening. A germ went

25

through her nose into her throat." Anna feels she disregarded the old timer's tale of not holding or breathing on infants because of germs.

The time for magical thinking began. First, the surrealism of the moment was not lost on Anna and her family. How could this possibly be true? Healthy pregnancy and birth, healthy child...should have, could have, would have. These magical thinking questions often help delay the reality until we are ready to accept the death. Anna explains that Amanda's christening was on one weekend and the Mass of the Angels on the next.

According to Anna, "it was so long ago but sometimes it seems like yesterday. My life has never been the same. I live day to day, bearing the heartache. I smile but most [people] don't know the toll the loss of a child has on your soul. I like when people remember her."

So, dear readers, let's remember Amanda and all the children who died too soon, whether through abortion, miscarriage, stillborn, or illness, and to the mothers who will celebrate this Valentine's Day by decorating the gravestones of their children with the hearts and flowers that they will never receive.

The Death of a Pet

B enjamin was a 60-something-year-old man. When he called me for an appointment, he made it clear he only wanted one session. He was a large man, tall and well-built, a man who might intimidate by both his size and demeanor. Ben spoke with a clipped speech, stern, and goal-oriented. He dismissed the formalities and got right down to his business at hand.

He told me his story as if he were reading the financial pages in the local newspaper.

"I am a single, retired man, no children, just my dog Captain, a seven-year-old black Lab. Captain slept in bed with me, traveled in my truck, and sat with pride in the passenger seat. We ate dinner, watched television, and hiked together. Never kept him on a leash – he was always glued to my side.

"Last week I offered to help paint a friend's house. It was a beautiful day. I climbed up the ladder and Captain sat in the grass, a sentinel at the first rung. I remember talking to him as I painted. "It's a great day to be alive, Captain. Look at the sky!

When we're finished, we'll go out for lunch and a run. Okay, buddy? Okay, Captain?" I expected a response, maybe a happy yelp or an enthusiastic bark. When I was met with silence, I looked down to see his facial expression, anticipating his wide-eyed, tail-wagging response to my plan. He wasn't there.

"At that very moment I heard a loud bang, a car horn beeping incessantly, and tires screeching. The driver on this quiet two-lane, country road was also enjoying the day and didn't see Captain standing in the middle of the street.

"Captain died immediately upon impact. The driver apologized profusely and kept repeating 'He never moved. He sat in the middle of the road and never moved. He saw me coming. He heard me coming and he NEVER MOVED!'"

At the conclusion of his story, Ben locked eyes with me. He began to sob, and eventually weep, and asked me through his tears, "I am here to ask you one question. Did Captain commit suicide? All the signs seem to indicate so. I thought he was happy. I thought I gave him a good life. Maybe I was wrong.

"If not, why did he cross the rainbow bridge at such a young age?"

Although dogs do experience depression, their survival instinct will usually be stronger. A dog's brain functions around the same level of a two-and-a-half-year-old child. We know that at this age, children have no concept of death; there is no evidence that dogs do either. (PsychologyToday.com)

I informed Ben of the research and was able to answer his question. "No, he did not commit suicide. I can't tell you why he chose not to move when he saw and/or heard the car coming, but he did not intentionally choose to die. As you expressed,

Ben, Captain lived a content and dignified life, full of love and companionship."

For the first and only time, Ben smiled. He stood, shook my hand, and thanked me. I never heard from him again.

The death of a pet can be equivalent to the loss of a loved one. In fact, the loss of a pet may be a greater loss than that of a loved one, depending on the relationship. Bonds with our pets are very intimate, as pets are non-judgmental, provide unconditional love, and are our biggest fans. They consistently show excitement upon seeing us, licking our faces and nudging us for a touch. People report taking time out of work to grieve their pet as the loneliness can be difficult. They are part of the family. There are pet cremation urns, and pet cemeteries, and Americans spend $72.56 billion yearly. (valuepenguin.com)

There is also a physiological reason for this bond. When we stroke or hug our pets, our brains release and increase oxytocin, the "feel good" hormone, and cortisol, "the stress hormone." In simple terms, pets make us feel good and reduce our stress. What is amazing is that this is reciprocal. Our pets' brains do the same – our touch increases oxytocin and reduces their anxiety. It is a mutually beneficial relationship, as anyone reading this knows.

Now go and snuggle your best friend. You are loved.

911

As a husband and a father of two small boys, David prided himself on being the man of the family. This included all the decision-making and problem-solving that a young family faces. Sometimes his need to have power and control caused a bit of a riff, but his wife Miranda usually understood his needs and often acquiesced to keep the peace.

David was a great dad who loved his boys and spent a great deal of time with them. Miranda was responsible for the cooking and cleaning and worked full-time in a demanding job. She was often tired. And so was David. Unusually tired. Miranda encouraged David to see his doctor. Perhaps it was low blood sugar, a simple vitamin deficiency or simply working too hard. David was a strong, athletic, active man of 42 and he rejected Miranda's advice. "There is nothing wrong with me. I'm not going to waste my time going to the doctor. I'm fine. I'm just tired."

A few months passed and David still exhibited increasing exhaustion. He often took afternoon naps on the couch, which was unusual, but despite Miranda's constant recommendations to see a doctor he declined. One afternoon, David was late coming home. When he finally showed up a few hours late, he told Miranda that he was so tired, he had pulled off to the side of the road and taken a nap in the car. Miranda's gentle, prodding recommendations now morphed into a demand. "David, you must go to the doctor. Something is wrong." Again, David declined, and Miranda felt helpless. He was a grown man and she couldn't make him do anything.

Weeks went by, the seasons changed, and David was now spending almost all of his time either in bed or on the couch. His activities with the boys diminished. Miranda's Google search of David's symptoms revealed a diagnosis she had not yet entertained. Depression. She thought, *if I can't get David to a medical doctor, how am I going to get him to a therapist or a prescription for anti-depressants?* Miranda chose a quiet time to share her thoughts with David. The boys were tucked in and sleeping soundly, and David seemed much less assertive and demanding as he had in the past. "David, I'm very concerned about your exhaustion. You can't even go to work you are so tired. Maybe it's not something physical. Do you think you might be depressed about something?"

Despite his lethargy, David responded with his familiar mantra. "I am fine. I am just tired. I am NOT depressed. If you are even thinking of sending me to a shrink, well, get it out of your mind right now. I am an adult and I can make my own choices. Don't tell me what to do."

Miranda cowered out of the room and resigned herself to the fact that David was never going to listen to her. He would go when he felt like it.

31

Some days later David was particularly exhausted, and as he lay on the couch he shouted, "Miranda, come here! I don't feel well!" Miranda ran into the room, frightened by the tone of David's voice. He sounded as if he was pleading. "David, I'm calling the rescue right now." "DON'T YOU DARE CALL 911," David shouted. "Just sit with me." So, she did. When it became too uncomfortable to watch him, as he seemed he was now in pain, Miranda went upstairs. She needed a mindless diversion. She watched a sitcom, took a few big breaths, and went back downstairs. David was in bad shape. "Miranda, call 911." She did. She always did what David told her to do.

He died of a massive heart attack on route to the hospital.

Miranda was angry at herself for not calling 911 hours ago. She was angry with David for refusing to get help. She was angry because she always did what he said.

And the boys? Children grieve differently at various developmental stages. When her youngest, Joshua, asked where Daddy went, Miranda told him, "He's in heaven." "No, he's not. His car is in the driveway." When she took the boys to the cemetery, Josh queried, "Is dad in the ground?" As Miranda responded "yes," Josh was already running to the truck to get a shovel. "Well, let's just dig him up!" Josh responded enthusiastically. He felt that he discovered the solution and was going to bring his daddy back.

At the very early age of two, Josh displayed "concreteness," an inability to reason in the abstract, although at age five his older brother Jonathan could. Jonathan didn't quite understand death, but he knew his daddy was not coming back.

As the weeks went by, Miranda noticed changes in the boys' behaviors. They were both very clingy and needed to have her in their sight. She couldn't use the bathroom or take a shower when the boys were home, as they would insist on joining her. She stopped her daily run. Both boys struggled with sleep and acting-out behavior. Miranda was seeing me, but she begged for some help for her boys. I referred her to Friends Way, the only organization in Rhode Island for grieving children. The boys did attend their respective age group activities once a week while Miranda took a seat upstairs with the other parents. I spoke with Miranda today and asked about her thoughts on Friends Way. "Friends Way has been amazing! The boys have learned how to recognize emotions and have gained coping mechanisms for handling them emotions."

There is comfort in harmony, simpatico, and sharing.

A Letter to My Father

Waiting for Dad

This is my 17th Father's Day without you, and it still feels like it was yesterday. I miss you, Dad.

As a young girl, I remember my frustration at having to wait until you came home from work before we were allowed to eat dinner. I thought it was unfair. Mom's nightly mantra was, "Your father works to pay for the food on this table. It's only fair to wait for him."

"But Mom, it's nine p.m. – almost bedtime and we are still waiting for Dad!"

Did you know this, Dad?

I spent a great deal of time waiting for you, Dad. Not just for dinner. Your work hours were unreliable and during our family summers at the beach house, you would drive down for the weekends. I looked forward to those weekends. I waited for you. Chasing rabbits with the car, your high beams on so we could follow them in the darkness that were the old tunnels at Fort Greene. Scary and exciting.

Do you remember my sleepover at the beach house? All my friends at the pajama party were enthralled with your antics. You were always so funny and fun.

Remember the one summer I was lucky enough to drive back to the city with you every Monday morning? I had to take driver's education. We always stopped at Snoopy's Diner for breakfast. A rare treat, just father and daughter. I hope you appreciated this special time as well.

Remember your Friday nights out with the boys, waking us all up upon your return with live lobsters crawling around the kitchen floor? You were always a prankster.

I loved to hear Nanny tell stories of you as a young boy. She always bragged about your intelligence, citing the fact that you skipped two grades. I was in awe! Remember the day you came home late, and Nanny was worried about you? You eventually showed up, but with a pony in tow!

You could be tough though, Dad. Particularly with boyfriends – none that really met with your standards for your only daughter.

And your laugh! You had such an infectious one – just listening to you laugh resulted in a cacophony of hysterics — although no one knew what we were laughing about, including us!

Even towards the end, when Parkinson's Disease had taken its toll, you were self-deprecating. You continued to golf, and your friends would tell us that you fell out of the golf cart and rolled down the hill, laughing the entire time!

Seriously though, Dad. At a very early age, you instilled in me the value of education and a philosophy of my place in the world.

"Mari, there is no such word as 'can't,' only 'won't.'"

I'm not sure if you ever realized how I took that philosophy to heart, and repeated it thousands of times to my students, my children, and my clients. I've used it as a driving force in life and work. Thank you for that.

I still wait for you, Dad. You've come to me in my grief dreams, dressed in a belted, khaki raincoat, offering me a home-made custard pie. I feel your presence whenever I smell your cigar wafting from downstairs in my home, or your cologne on someone sitting next to me at the movies.

On really difficult days, I wear your old bathrobe — you know the teal, brushed cotton one? I still have your grey running shorts as well. They are big, but when needed I roll up the waist a few times. Just once in a while. Once in a while I look at old pictures and think about how the family has grown. You have four great-grandchildren now. Your grandsons work at the funeral home along with your sons. I am still teaching, working with clients, and volunteering. Whenever I'm confronted with a choice, I ask myself, "Is this a 'can't' or a 'won't'?" And if my response is "can't," I hear your voice, loud and clear, and know that I can. Always. You would be proud.

Happy Birthday and Happy Father's Day to my dad.

Death Ends a Life, Not a Relationship

"The waiting is the hardest part
Every day you see one more card
You take it on faith, you take it to the heart
The waiting is the hardest part."
(Tom Petty and The Heartbreakers,
"The Waiting," from the album *Hard Promises*, 1981)

Sarah was ten years old when her fourth-grade teacher gave the class an assignment. Sister Gertrude walked up and down the aisles of desks, and as she walked she offered each student an opportunity to choose one of thirty envelopes that sat in the basket she carried.

"Each one of you will choose an envelope that contains the name and address of another young person from a different country. The name you choose will be your pen pal!"

Sarah was quite excited for this novel English assignment. Several students rifled through the envelopes to access the choices before picking one. Sarah was a curious and gifted child who loved to read and write. She closed her eyes and reached up and into the basket. She believed in fate. Her envelope had the name "Patrick" written in Sister Gertrude's Palmer Method penmanship, along with an address – Kerry, Ireland. In retrospect, Sarah remembers how exotic the idea of writing to Patrick from Ireland was in her ten-year-old mind. She dashed home from the bus stop that same afternoon, and wrote her first letter to Patrick.

Dear Patrick, My name is Sarah Jones. I am 10 years old and live in a pretty town in Massachusetts, USA. I have one sister and 2 cats, Portia and Phoebe. My mom is a teacher. My dad is a carpenter. I am very excited to meet you. Please write back soon. Sarah

Even though her mom told her it would be quite a while before she received a response, Sarah checked the mailbox religiously. Every day. Her mom showed her where Kerry was on the globe, and traced a finger from New England to Ireland.

"Sarah, do you see how far your letter has to travel? Patrick's letter needs to travel the same distance back."

Sarah tried to busy herself with after-school activities: jump rope, bicycling with her friends, playing hide and seek and tag – all in an effort to appease her impatience. The waiting is the hardest part.

One Wednesday, as Sarah checked the mailbox for the third time that day, she noticed a crumpled-up yellow envelope merged between the pile of bills and grocery flyers. It was addressed to her, with a return address of Kerry, Ireland.

Dear Sarah – We have the same assignment. I thought a boy would pick me but I'm glad you did. I liked your letter. I have one sister and many sheep and cows. It is very green here with lots of room to run and play. Please write back and send a picture. Patrick

Thus began a lifelong correspondence between the two. They did indeed share school pictures, every year, and during adolescence Sarah remembers a "bit of a crush on both sides." Their letters contained the happenings of the day in their respective countries, families, and school. Eventually they both went off to local colleges. The letters were consistent but the news sparse; however, each of their letters expressed a desire to meet in person someday. After college, both Sarah and Patrick married someone they had met in college. Yet the letter writing continued. As time went on, the pictures morphed into proud parents of newborns, then toddlers, weddings, and finally family pictures with grandchildren surrounding them. They spoke of their parents who had passed, a granddaughter who was taking ballet, a grandson who played soccer.

The letters span over 50 years.

Recently Sarah's husband passed and she poured her grief out to Patrick. His wife had passed a few years back. Now, with both of them in their late sixties, they agreed it was finally time to meet. Sarah would fly to Kerry and Patrick and his sister, Colleen, would meet Sarah at the airport.

Sarah attempted to explain her anticipation, excitement, and dread to me. The prospect of meeting Patrick after all these years filled her with a flurry of emotions and anxiety. Never lovers but best friends and confidantes, Sarah prepared for the trip. She kept each and every one of his letters, which she packed in a satchel to prove to him that she had indeed saved all his correspondence. She boarded the plane, put her smartphone on airplane mode, and slept most of the flight, with the help of a few martinis and memories of reading *Griffin and Sabine*.

She missed the text. When she arrived at the airport, Sarah recognized Colleen coming toward her through the throngs of travelers. Sarah thought she looked upset. There was no sign of Patrick. Teary-eyed, Colleen approached Sarah and wrapped her arms around her.

"Father passed on this morning. It was very sudden. A massive heart attack."

Sarah fell to the ground, as travelers stopped to help her and airport security came to assist in what they perceived as a medical crisis. Sarah had fainted. The irony was not lost on Sarah. After fifty-plus years in a relationship with someone she considered her soul mate, a man she told all of the mundane as well as all of her inner most thoughts and secrets to, the confidante she was finally about to meet and hug – was gone. Although neither had left a word unsaid, there was great sadness in the fact that they had never truly met.

Colleen never married and kept up the family farm. Sarah accompanied Colleen to the family home where Patrick had lived as a child – where he had written that first letter in his ten-year-old handwriting.

Sarah attended Patrick's wake and funeral. As she knelt at the casket she stroked his cold cheek, and ran her fingers through his hair. She said a prayer and then whispered in his ear,

> *"We gather today to mourn*
> *We'll meet again before too long*
> *We can question why you were called*
> *Remember God has a plan for us all*
> *Hello Patrick*
> *Hello Patrick*
> *Hello Patrick, I just came to say goodbye*
>   (Dean Petrella & Joe Matira,
>   lyricists, from "Hello Dawn," 2020)

Following the priest's prayers at the cemetery, throngs of people gathered for the collation at the family farm. Sarah recognized many people from the pictures Patrick had sent. She recalled many other names from the stories Patrick had shared.

When everyone had depleted the vast amounts of food and beer, they left, leaving Colleen and Sarah alone in the house. Both women were silent, quiet in their own personal reveries as they sat in the family sitting room. Sarah was thinking of the satchel of letters she brought to show Patrick. Colleen was thinking, *Should I share something with her?*

Finally, Colleen interrupted the silence.

"Sarah, would you like to see my brother's childhood room? He has visited it many times over the years, but always locks the door when he leaves. If he were here, I think he would want you to…"

Sarah agreed, and tentatively followed Colleen up the stairs and down a hallway to a door facing them.

Colleen knew where her brother kept the key. She had always known. She unlocked the door and stood aside for Sarah to enter. Sarah gasped and lost her breath, only for a moment, as the bittersweet view came into focus. Patrick had wallpapered his entire bedroom with each and every one of Sarah's letters. From her very first letter, written for an English assignment to a ten-year-old boy from Kerry, Ireland, to her most recent announcement containing her flight information.

It was the loveliest, heart-breaking tribute to Sarah. Sarah returned home to mourn the loss of both her husband and Patrick. She wrapped herself in her husband's old sweater as she opened her satchel and gingerly and lovingly took out Patrick's letters. Slowly and methodically she began to wallpaper her room.

High Tech Takes Its Role in Grieving

The face of funeral arrangements has evolved; even the choices of burial methods are now wide and varied. Next week I will discuss all these choices and the fact that it is never too early to make arrangements. Today I chose to share a personal experience that I believe will become more common moving forward in the preparation of wakes and funerals.

I entered the wake of Anna, an eighty-something-year-old woman who in life was never seen without a cigarette in her mouth and an oxygen tank by her side. Hers was an expected death and the tone of the room was less than somber. I paused at the kneeler, said the obligatory prayer, and said my goodbyes to Auntie. The first in the receiving line was her sister, a sweet attractive woman struggling with Alzheimer's disease, but today her mind's eye was with us. She accepted my condolences with a pleasant smile as I continued along. Next in line were Anna's two nieces and I spoke with them. I noticed and wondered why a group of people were huddled around the next chair in the receiving line. They all seemed to be looking down as if speaking with a child.

As the small crowd dispersed, I was finally able to determine the cause of all the commotion. Sitting in a large, high-backed upholstered chair of greens and blues was an iPad. I was taken aback, but crouched down to view the screen. The image of Anna's son addressed me. "Hello, and thank you for coming," he said, via Skype. I remained crouched down with my hands on my knees as I responded, "So sorry about your mom." The iPad was last in the receiving line.

As I mingled through the small crowd of visitors, I overheard the older people complaining, emphatic about not talking to a computer. It seems her son, Ralphie, was currently living in the Philippines and decided that a long, expensive flight was uncalled for, given the threat of Ebola at the time, and the inevitability of his chain-smoking, oxygen-dependent mother's death.

Ralphie attended the funeral Mass as well. From any vantage point in the church, the image of the iPad held high above a friend's head was unavoidable. And, given that it was a Catholic Mass, the iPad received communion.

I can't help but wonder if, in the near future, virtual attendance will be *de rigueur*. Perhaps funeral homes should consider supplying iPads as part of the funeral package along with the traditional DVD of the deceased person's life.

$\mathcal{H}$oliday $\mathcal{S}$tress $\mathcal{T}$ips for $\mathcal{G}$rievers $\mathcal{H}$elp $\mathcal{U}$s $\mathcal{A}$ll

According to the Holmes-Rahe Stress Inventory (1967), which lists 43 life events with a corresponding stress point value level in order to measure your level of stress, you will garner 12 points just for holiday gatherings.

Yes, holidays cause stress for a host of different reasons. Add holiday preparation to your daily juggling of activities and you may experience stress overload. Stress is a part of our "hurry up" society where we become overwhelmed with too much incoming stimulation. The fight or flight response is alive and well for those of us who wait in long lines at the cash registers or wake early for Black Friday and Cyber Monday. The holiday season is fraught with a frenzy of activity: gift purchases, food preparation, and decorations.

For grievers, it's a reminder of a finite or non-finite loss. A finite loss includes the loss of a family member whose place at the holiday table remains empty. A non-finite loss is the "ongoing sense of guilt" (Bruce & Shultz, 2003) associated with a non-death loss: a job, a marriage, a disenfranchised child.

Social media and television commercials paint a joyous season of love and laughter. When we feel anger rather than joy, sadness instead of love, we feel guilty. All these emotions alone or combined are a recipe for stress and anxiety. Anxiety can be a physiological reaction to stress. We may experience high blood pressure or blood pressure spikes, digestive issues, sleep impairment, headaches, shingles, and heart palpitations. Oftentimes our attempts to ameliorate these symptoms includes the use of alcohol and drugs. These are not only ineffective but may exacerbate the symptoms. Here are a few effective methods to deal with holiday stress:

1. Give yourself permission. In our quest to be perfect and to do everything right, we invite stress. Give yourself permission to take time, take a breath. Inhale, exhale, and breathe. Do your gift shopping during the slow shopping times, usually between five and seven in the evening.

2. Slow down. The popular method of mindfulness encourages us to stay in the moment, rather than focusing on the past and the future. Give yourself permission to leave the wrapping or the dishes for 20 minutes and use one of the many mindfulness/meditation apps for smartphones. You may also do a bit of yoga, take a short walk, or listen to soothing music. Having a pet is a bonus – by petting your dog you both release oxytocin – the "feel good" hormone that will be mutually beneficial.

3. The use of aromatics (particularly lavender), light jazz, salt lamps, and an adult coloring book can calm the stress beast very quickly.

4. Take care of yourself. Stress breaks down your immune system and will wreak havoc. Eat small, high-protein food and snacks 4-6 times a day. Find your favorite method to unwind before bedtime. Avoid watching television in bed.

5. Stay away from excessive use of wine or sleep aids.

6. If you are grieving, give yourself permission to grieve during the holidays. You will hear many well-meaning individuals give you advice that angers you. If this is the year of "firsts" after the death of a loved one, prepare yourself for the onslaught of tears. Research indicates that tears are self-soothing and contain cortisol, a stress hormone, so as you cry you are releasing stress. Follow the steps outlined above. Some choose to set an empty place and raise a glass in celebration of a life well lived.

7. Repeat. Take care of yourself. Make your self-care a priority, which provides you with the health and wellness to enjoy the holiday season.

A Good Time for an Angel Story
To Cindy

"…There's a time that I remember when I never felt so lost
When I felt all of the hatred was too powerful to stop
Now my heart feels like an ember
And it's lighting up the dark
I'll carry these torches for ya
That you know I'll never drop…
Cheers to the wish you were here, but you're not
Cause the [dreams] bring back all the memories
And the memories bring back
Memories bring back you."
(Maroon 5, "Memories," 2019)

A dear client of mine, Cindy, lived with her daughter, Sarah, and two grandchildren (Anthony, age 13, and Adrian, age 6), as she waited to die. Cindy was diagnosed with multisystem failure and was told she had less than six months to live. She was 53 years old. She seized every one of those remaining days and filled them with a bucket list of to-dos: A ride to Galilee for chowder and clam cakes, a convertible drive on Route 95 north going nowhere, listening to 60's and 70's tunes as she blasted them for the edification of every passer-by, despite the speed. As her end of life grief counselor, I was fortunate enough to be the chosen one that accompanied her as she checked off the boxes. The last box to check touched my heart the most. Her last request included a presentation to my college counseling class, whose content included a discussion of both the process of death and the process of counseling. Cindy had been an addictions counselor before she fell ill.

It was early fall when Cindy stood at the podium in my class while her presentation was videotaped. She wanted to "live on forever in the Counseling department at JWU," and I promised her I would show her video to each of my classes for as long as I taught. And I have. My students hold on to Cindy's mantra about therapy:

"Therapists need to have the skin of a rhinoceros and the heart of a dove."

Indeed, we do.

Cindy passed during the holiday season in the hospice hospital. Her daughter and grandchildren could no longer take care of her as she was failing quickly. They lived on the second floor of a tenement on a busy city road, too difficult for Cindy to maneuver. She donated her body to Brown University Medical Center.

A few months after Cindy's death, our state was blanketed with, as little Adrian would later describe it, "a great big snowstorm! The kind that closed schools and gives you enough snow for a family of snowmen and a huge igloo for a house! It was up to my waist!!"

Unfortunately, the power went out and the family lit some scented candles to shed some light on the tiny apartment. In short, one of the candles inadvertently got knocked over in the den area. By the time Sarah noticed the smell of smoke, several of the items in the den had caught on fire. Within minutes the entire apartment was in flames. Sarah grabbed both Anthony and Adrian, who were both barefoot, in their pajamas ready for bed, and hustled them down the stairs, to the frigid cold and snow outside.

They successfully made it out of the house in time to watch it burn to the ground. They were freezing, barefoot, and without jackets. There wasn't time. The main thoroughfare was empty and unplowed, and with parking restrictions, there were no cars in sight.

Both the fire department and the Red Cross responded, but not before Sarah noticed an old woman walking down the main street, slowly but with purpose. As she approached the family, she said, "Oh my, I was just in town to view an art exhibit. I'm from Boston. I know what it is like to be a victim of a fire and lose everything one has. In fact, I am always prepared for a fire since my experience."

Sarah and the children looked at her, blinking over and over. Where did she come from? Where is her car? Who is she?"

The woman's name was Edna. Edna indicated she would be right back as she went to retrieve her car. The family watched her walk back down the empty main street and turn a corner. Within minutes a car came crawling up the unplowed main street, skidding to a slow stop just past the house in flames.

Edna proceeded to get out of the car and opened her trunk. The trunk was stuffed full of garbage bags. From those bags Edna pulled out winter jackets, hats, socks, gloves, and boots. She also had an assortment of blankets. The family was both grateful and shocked. Shortly after, the fire trucks arrived and put out the flames, leaving a charred outline of what once was. The Red Cross was next to arrive and provided the family with drinks and snacks, along with a voucher for a hotel room.

Edna remained and drove the family to the hotel. Of course, the family was beyond grateful, despite the loss of all their possessions and belongings, as well as the recent loss of Cindy.

A few weeks later, I called Sarah to tell her I had a check from Hospice for her family. She invited me over to her father's house, where they had temporarily set up living quarters.

When I arrived, Sarah and the children were excited to show me a once-empty bedroom. When they opened the door, I was surprised to see a room stocked floor to ceiling with winter clothes of all sizes, books, and toys galore. Sarah told me that Edna had set up a foundation at her Boston office and all the employees sent donations.

The family could not fathom their good fortune. Who was Edna? And how did it come to pass that she was walking alone, down a deserted, unplowed street? Was there actually an art exhibit that hadn't been cancelled? Did the fire serve as a beacon for her? And where did she go? Once she dropped the family off at the hotel, she disappeared. The only evidence of her presence were the clothes on their backs and the warmth of the blankets. And the presents. Sent from strangers in Boston.

P.S. Cindy, I know you sent Edna!

Or…perhaps it was you in Edna's body. Maybe God let you leave heaven for a bit to visit earth and help your family. I write this article in your honor. We remember you always. Your family lost all the family pictures and any sign of your existence, including all your clothes, but we all hold onto the memories of you. They cannot be destroyed. Or burned.

Oh, and by the way, I recently found your black cardigan sweater in my back seat, you know the one you brought on our convertible ride in case it got cold? I'm going to give it to Sarah.

It still holds your scent. Rest in peace, my dear friend.

Part 2

Dealing with a Pandemic

SEVEN STORIES

Beauty in the Broken Places, A Covid Love Story

Our collective hearts are broken with the loss of Ray and Joan Connery. They met on a Cape Cod beach and within a year, they married. Five children, seven grandchildren, four great-grandchildren, and 66 years of marriage later, they both died at the age of 93 from COVID.

Ray was a veteran of the Navy and a retired lieutenant with the Rhode Island State Police. Following his retirement, he worked as the chief security officer at Eastland Bank in Woonsocket – and served on the North Smithfield Town Council for 10 years.

Ray was equally well known for his gardens, his golf game, and his baked stuffed mushrooms. He loved to create large batches of clam chowder from quahogs he dug himself. Ray lived a full and purposeful life, replete with his love of both the Red Sox and the Patriots. Ray maintained a strong will and determination to live and serve. He lived and loved with both integrity and dignity as he sustained a deep and abiding faith. Above all, Ray was Joan's best friend. And Joan was the love of his life.

Joan was chief dietician of Woonsocket Hospital before leaving to start their family. Joan then went on to pursue a degree in education and taught for 22 years as the reading specialist and director of literacy in North Smithfield. She also taught English as a second language to Vietnamese children and established her legacy as the founder of the "Read to Me" program at Hasbro Children's Hospital.

Ray and Joan lived a loving and fulfilled life as they traveled via Elderhostel. Joan loved the color purple and chocolates, and Ray taught many a grandchild the art of eating sun-warmed raspberries right off the bush.

My snapshot memories include Ray and Joan and our shared love of the ocean, the Rhode Island coastline, and making new and fast friends. We were fortunate to be included as some of their new, fast friends. Ray and Joan, along with their daughter, joined us as we sailed on Narragansett Bay on blessed summer days.

Ray, with his quick wit, mischievous twinkle in his eye, and Joan, a hardy mate who fed on the history of the homes on the coast, graced the cockpit of the *Raven*. We are so grateful to Susan for sharing her parents with us.

Their last days were spent apart, with Ray hospitalized in the surgical intensive care unit and Joan a few doors down in a room on the COVID unit. They were in contact with their family solely through the use of modern technology. Only in Joan's last days did she reunite with her family. Their final days were bittersweet: they died within 22 days of each other, and now are forever united. We are blessed for having shared a small portion of their lives, even in our broken places.

Rest in peace, Ray and Joan Connery

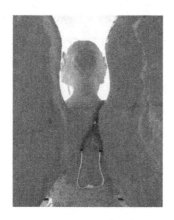

Pandemic Memories – Nurses Know Best

"I prayed to God today,
A sudden, selfish choice.
I kneeled down to pray today
He didn't recognize my voice."
(Lyrics by Dean Petrella of The Complaints)

My clients frequently report that this quarantine has allowed for far too much time alone to think without distraction. One client described it as "a scrying mirror for the mind's demons to resurrect." This is what happened with Marjorie. She heard the reports of children dying in New York with atypical COVID-19 symptoms that mimicked Kawasaki disease. It was the word "Kawasaki" that triggered a traumatic memory, which she shares below.

"I wish I could disremember this, Dr. D. I tried, but I can't seem to erase the fear. Can you help me? These are my memories. (deep inhale and sigh) Austin was a healthy, active, and bright 12-year-old boy. It was January, the height of the flu season that year. I remember like it was this morning. I know because I was there. I am his mom.

"Austin came home from school on a Thursday, saying that he didn't feel well and collapsed on his bed face first, still in his winter coat and burdensome backpack. I let him sleep for a while. When I went back to check on him, his forehead burned my hand. I woke him, gave him Tylenol, and continued to wake him throughout the night, alternating Tylenol and Motrin in what I would soon realize was a desperate, and ultimately failed attempt.

"The following morning, a Friday, he still had a fever of 102, and refused to eat or drink anything. He wanted more sleep. I called my neighbor, a primary care physician, and described the situation. 'Oh, he just has the flu. All five of my kids are just getting over it. Just keep him hydrated, maintain the medication regimen for the fever, and he'll be fine,' the doctor responded.

"I pleaded with him. 'Steve, I would feel better if you just ran over to check on him. He's never sick.'

"'No need Marjorie, it's just the flu.'

"I felt uneasy. Something didn't feel quite right, but I couldn't put my proverbial finger on it. I decided to take Austin to the local walk-in treatment center. His stubborn fever remained at 102, and he appeared pale and weak. He leaned on me as we walked to the car, and then again when we arrived at the treatment center.

"We met Dr. Forester, who after a full examination, seemed to agree with my neighbor, Steve.

"'It appears to be a just a bad case of the flu. But let's do some blood work just in case.'

"'Just in case of what?' I thought.

"We returned home, Austin to another night of a medication regimen and I, slipping the thermometer through his parched, cracked lips as he slept. Any attempt to hydrate him proved futile, as he vomited after one swallow.

"My unease segued to an easy panic: a second sleepless night for me sitting in the darkness, waiting for daylight, and praying for a reprieve from his fever. No luck. The phone rang on Saturday's sunrise, an ominous sign. It was Dr. Forester.

"'Good morning, Marjorie. I just received Austin's blood work results, which cause me some concern. How is his fever?'

"'Still one hundred and two. It hasn't changed since Thursday night.'

"'Well, my concern is this: his blood bands are very high. This means that he has a serious bacterial infection, or a virus, probably the flu. You see, when our body is attacked by a virus our white blood cell counts increase, preparing to fight off the virus. When the white blood cells aren't strong enough, or there aren't enough of them to fight, the body sends a signal to the bone marrow to release more white blood cells. Sending in more troops, so to speak. I suggest you call his pediatrician or take him to a hospital emergency room. At the minimum, he is sure to need intravenous fluid as you can tell he is getting extremely dehydrated.'

"I left my house quickly. My panic became uneasy. I weaved in and out of traffic, well over the speed limit and returned home. I called the pediatrician only to hear a recording: 'To all our patients, if you missed the notice in your local newspaper, Dr. B has retired. All medical records can be re-trieved by writing to the following address....'

"My uneasy panic blossomed to a full-blown adrenaline rush. I called my neighbor. Remember him? Steve the primary care physician? I explained the details of what had occurred since we last spoke. I told him about the blood bands. This time I begged.

"'Please come and examine him! His pediatrician retired. I have few options and he's not getting any better!' I was frantic and determined.

"'No need. It's just the flu. If it makes you feel better, take him to the hospital emergency room. But don't take him to Hasbro Children's Hospital – you'll be in the waiting room for hours. Take him to a local hospital.'

"So I did. By the time we reached a very quiet, unpopu-lated local hospital emergency room, Austin had to be carried. He was so weak. The bone marrow troops didn't seem adequate. Fortunately, we were greeted by a gregarious, loquacious, young doctor – short, stocky, and extremely confident. He im-mediately gave my son an IV rehydration, and after a short time Austin claimed that he felt 'a little bit better.' He was pinking up a bit. The doctor assured us that it was the flu and now that he was hydrated, he would continue to feel better.

"He assured me again, 'If you have any continued con-cerns or questions, please don't hesitate to come back.'

"I sighed with a bit of relief and a subtle yet persistent, unrelenting *je ne sais quoi*. The relief dissipated immediately when the nurse who signed us out took one look at the chart and took me aside.

"'Marjorie,' she said, 'I don't mean to scare you, but your son is very sick. I worked in the pediatric intensive care unit at Hasbro Children's Hospital for fifteen years. I don't know what he has, but he is very ill. If he doesn't show improvement by tomorrow, bring him right back here.'

"That persistent, unrelenting feeling roared. 'But the doctor just said....'

"She interrupted me. 'Listen to what I just said. Bring him back.'

"This is what psychologists refer to as an avoidance-avoidance conflict. It was, I thought at the time, the worst night of my life. Austin's fever still maintained at one hundred and two, and on Sunday morning, he woke with a strange new symptom. It looked as if he had dipped both his hands in red paint. Upon further inspection, I noticed that his eyelids and below his eyes were pink. As I tried to lift him out of the bed to get his coat on, the phone rang.

"It was the nurse.

"She sounded out of breath. 'Marjorie, how is Austin this morning?'

"I filled her in on the new symptoms.

"'I am so sorry I wasn't as emphatic yesterday as I had planned. You see, I had to say something, but I didn't say enough. I couldn't sleep last night, and I can't look myself in the mirror. Your son is very, very ill. Please bring him back to the ER. I am here.'

"When we arrived for the second time, the same gregarious, loquacious, confident doctor was on call. Today he was a short, stocky, Machiavelli.

"He shouted at me. 'What are you doing back here already?'

"His booming, cocky voice did not intimidate me. I was on fire. I was a mother on the warpath who trusted the nurse above all else. My intuition told me so.

"'Well, you told me to come back if I had any additional concerns or questions,' I replied in a mocking imitation. 'I simply want you to rule some other conditions out.'

"He became even more belligerent. He grabbed my son's head and began to shake it vigorously.

"'What, rule out meningitis?' He continued to shout and shake Austin's head. Then he took his fingers and held Austin's eyes as wide as he was able. 'What, rule out hepatitis?' His voice was now escalating.

"With every mention of a new condition his anger escalated exponentially. He seemed to snarl when he finished.

"'HE HAS THE FLU! WHAT PART DO YOU NOT UNDERSTAND?!'

"'Might you admit him?'

"'NO.'

"'Might you refer him to Hasbro?'

"'NO.'

"'Call a rescue to take him there?'

"'NO.'

"I replied, calmly and confidently, 'Doctor, when we left last evening, the nurse told me he was very ill and to return if he seemed worse. He does. He has bright red hands and pink circles around his eyes.'

"He looked as if he was going to burst. 'A nurse! A NURSE! Who? Which one?'

"He proceeded to round up all the nurses and put them in an identification line-up. All that was missing were the numbers on a card. My nurse would have been number five.

"He addressed number one. 'Was it YOU?'

"'No, doctor.'

"He addressed number two.

"'Was it you?'

"He was pacing back and forth with his arms behind his back, bullying them like an inquisitor.

"My number five nurse took a step forward.

"'I was the one.'

"He grabbed her by her sleeve and pulled her aside as I heard him vehemently shouting at her through the privacy curtain.

"'WHO DO YOU THINK YOU ARE? GOING OVER MY HEAD! SHE IS JUST A HYSTERICAL MOTHER. HE HAS THE FLU. YOU WILL BE SORRY YOU EVER SAID ANYTHING. I WILL REPORT YOU!'

"And with that he stomped off.

"We prepared to leave, and as we walked out to the parking lot, I heard footsteps running behind us. It was the nurse.

"'I'm so sorry,' she said. 'I could lose my job and my license, and I really can't afford to as I am a single mother with a disabled son. But my conscience is berating me. Get yourself to Hasbro Children's Hospital immediately.'

"Which we did.

"Our nurse had called ahead with our information and we were met at the door, where they scooped up my son out of my arms and rushed him to the back. IV rehydration and blood work were completed immediately, and they chose to admit him. The doctors and nurses were astounded that Austin presented with these grave symptoms and was discharged twice from another hospital. Finally, I felt safe. I was in the right place. I exhaled. They transferred him to a lovely, private room. I planned on spending another sleepless night as my son's sentinel. I am a mother, a watchful warrior.

"Shortly thereafter, a nurse came in the room to check his vital signs. As she pumped up the blood pressure cuff and waited, she appeared confused.

"'Oh my, this is not working. I will be right back with another.'

"She scurried off and returned with a brand-new blood pressure gauge.

"'Oh my, what are the chances of grabbing two faulty cuffs?!' she exclaimed. 'I'll be right back.'

"She returned for a third time without success. She hadn't completely left the room before an organized chaos ensued. A half dozen medical personnel arrived and addressed me in a calm, efficient tone.

"'Marjorie, your son's blood pressure is very low. So low it's not registering. We are here to transfer him to the Pediatric Intensive Care Unit. We will come back in about ten minutes to escort you there. Is there anyone you would like to call?'

"'Well, my mom. But my parents are in Florida,' I said.

"'CALL THEM' they shouted over their shoulders as they hurriedly transferred my son to a waiting gurney.

"I inhaled and held my breath.

"I walked into his ICU room. There were so many monitors and tubes and IV poles – he looked so small among all the equipment, like an unwilling participant in a covert medical experiment. They were pumping him with fluids to increase his blood pressure, which was initially successful. But there are often unintentional consequences. The influx of fluids brought his blood pressure up and caused pulmonary edema. When they stopped the fluids, the edema decreased and so did his blood pressure.

"The next few days? Weeks? They were like being on a merry-go-round, always missing the brass ring. The CDC doctors came in from Atlanta, dressed in personal protective equipment. I was obliged to dress the same as I never left his room. Was it contagious? What was it? Pediatric specialists from around New England were called to consult. There was no diagnosis. Spinal tap. Not meningitis.

"They asked if we had been traveling recently.

"'Yes,' I said, 'to London and Paris over Thanksgiving.'

"They ruled out mad cow disease, encephalitis, and West Nile virus. While my son lay dying.

"'Well, it could be atypical Kawasaki. Or atypical Adenovirus,' they mused, as they tsked and stared at each other.

"'Sorry. It's a mystery. Might he be the host of a new novel virus?'

"Austin's spleen was enlarged. The next day his kidneys were failing but the spleen was fine. His heart showed an arrythmia and then it didn't.

"I just kept waiting to exhale. And prayed. I prayed like I have never prayed before. I bargained, cajoled, begged God. I kept up my ongoing one-way dialogue with him. 'God, is this a punishment? God, tell me what you want me to do. I'll do anything. Just save my son.'

"And God finally recognized my voice. It came in the form of gamma globulin. Austin began to show improvement. Slowly. Methodically.

"He was allowed to go home. Finally. He wore a halter monitor to gauge his heart and kept up pediatric cardiology appointments for a few years. He went back to middle school for half days until he completely convalesced. Several months later, two young teens died with the same symptoms. Death certificates indicated the cause of death as the flu. Austin's final diagnosis was atypical adenovirus. His case was written up in the medical journals.

"I never heard back from my nurse, except for a card she sent upon his middle school graduation; however, I know she saved my son's life. The PICU nurses informed me that if I had returned home rather than going to Hasbro, my son would have died in his own bed that evening. His blood pressure would have bottomed out.

"Remember my neighbor, Steve? When he heard that Austin was in the PICU he was quoted as saying, 'Thank God I didn't go over to the house when she asked. I may have been culpable.'

"It has been rumored that the short, stocky Machiavellian doctor called the PICU in tears.

"I sued him. He was put on probation for six months while attorneys investigated.

"My son's files indicated that he was 'Referred to Hasbro for further evaluation.'

"The nurse lost her job, even after my lengthy deposition before the hospital board. I will never forget her name. I have conducted many online searches to no avail. She seems to have disappeared.

"Perhaps she was a guardian angel....

Missing That Human Touch

"Tell me in a world without pity
Do you think what I'm askin's too much?
I just want something to hold on to
And a little of that human touch
Just a little of that human touch"
(Bruce Springsteen, "Human Touch," 1992)

Unfortunately, lack of human touch, also known as "touch deprivation" or "skin hunger," is alive and well in our country. Benedict Carey identified this issue long before COVID-19. In his 2010 *New York Times* article entitled "Evidence that little touches do mean so much," Carey states, "We live in a country that's starved for physical affection, where an outbreak of hugging by high school students prompts media coverage and even alarm, when many other cultures would find it either unremarkable or worth celebrating."(www.nytimes.com/2010 /02/23/health/ 23mind.html)

Field in Jones, 2018 agrees and adds that with social media, and cell phones along with "no touch" policies in schools and therapy practices, we are touching each other less. And all this research is based on behavior before COVID-19!

Today, we arm ourselves with the weapon of social distancing against COVID-19 and forego touch. Many of my clients who struggle with anxiety and depression are actually grieving the loss of human touch. Studies show us that touch "signals safety and trust…as it triggers a release of oxytocin (the love hormone)". (Keltner, 2010) "During this time of necessary social distancing, lockdown, and isolation, I worry about my clients, society, and the future effects of this distancing in society" (Roberts, M. Covid-19, and Touch Deprivation, 2020). According to the Kansas Health Care Association (www.khca.org), "there are eight reasons why we need touch now more than ever:

1) touch decreases violence;

2) it provides greater trust between individuals;

3) it is associated with economic gain;

4) it builds a strong immune system;

5) it adds to stronger team dynamics;

6) it encourages more non-sexual emotional intimacy;

7) it provides greater learning engagement; and

8) it increases overall well-being."

Decades of research have shown us the importance of touch in the attachment of newborns to their caretakers. Today, pediatricians encourage not just touch, but skin-to-skin contact. That has not always been the case. In the early 1900's, Dr. Holt, a pediatrician, became concerned with the attention and the subsequent perceived "spoiling" of our children, and advocated for less touch. It wasn't until the death rates of healthy infants began to increase that the medical community identified the lack of touch as the cause of death.

A famous study conducted in the 1940's used an experimental research method with two groups of infants. One group was raised in a completely sterile environment, given adequate survival care of feeding, bathing, and dressing. The second group was provided with the same care supplemented with cuddling, hugging, and swaddled. Within four months of this study, almost one-half of the infants in the sterile environment died. The infants in the second group all faired fine and developed appropriately.

There were additional studies with monkeys (remember Harry Harlow and his infamous study of rhesus monkeys?). Newborns were separated from their mothers and given the option of two surrogate mothers: one a wire mesh monkey wrapped in a soft towel and the other with a bottle of milk. Unsurprisingly, the newborn monkeys chose the "mom" with the soft towel, opting for comfort rather than sustenance.

Other studies looked at "feral children" who were raised without touch and worked backwards. Take the case of Genie. Genie was locked in a room, tied to a potty chair for the majority of the day, and fed by her brother, who was warned not to speak to her. When Genie was 13 years old, social services discovered her existence and many professionals and foster families attempted to rehabilitate Genie. When she was found, she could not speak, was not toilet trained, and could only walk bent over with bowed legs, salivating, and urinating constantly. The sad results of these efforts can be found in Maya Pines famous article entitled "The Civilization of Genie" (1997) or the documentary *Secrets of a Wild Child*. Through this study we learn that touch is not only important to survival, but lack of it can cause developmental delays in psychological, neurological, physical, and intelligence factors.

Finally, the case of Isabelle seems to cement the argument for the need for human touch. Isabelle, discovered at age seven, had spent the first years of her life in an isolated, dark room with her deaf-mute mother as her only contact. Although Isabelle's mother could not hear or speak, she could hold her daughter. Within seven months of her rescue, Isabelle met the criteria for other children in her age group. Human touch insured her survival.

Rebekkah Mikkola is a "cuddle therapist" and can be seen in both her TEDx talk and on YouTube in "The Power of Touch," emphasizing the fact that touch decreases loneliness. Yet we are fearful of touching others during this pandemic. Some are paralyzed and/or stuck in this fear, unable to entertain the thought of touching a loved one. Several experts recommend a hot bath, a blanket, or hugging a pet as potential efforts in mimicking the human touch.

If we are lucky enough to live with loved ones and/or family, it is essential to touch and hug them. If you do not have access to pets or people, we should create circumstances by keeping our senses alive. "This can be accomplished by touching and feeling things with texture, polished stones, smooth wooden surfaces, soft toys, silk or fur. Pay more attention to how the shower feels on your body and the sensation of your clothes on your skin." (Roberts, 2020).

Fortunately for me, I have a 92-year-old mom who drives to the market to complete her grocery shopping, goes to CVS to pick up her prescriptions, has regular appointments with her hair and nail stylists, and is always willing to give and receive a hug. For that I am grateful.

I encourage all of you to put down your cell phones, shut off the television, and touch more. Hug or hold hands safely. If that is not possible, wrap your arms around yourself in a self-hug.

With touch you will survive the isolation and loneliness. With touch, you will survive and thrive.

NOTE: This article was written pre-vaccine. Currently it appears clients feel the same about the vaccine as they did the antibodies.

We Want Our Lives Back

How many of you believe that you had COVID-19 long before it was a household word?

Since my announcement a few weeks ago that GracePointe Grief offers free support services via telehealth, we have been inundated with calls. As expected, many concerns include anxiety, depression, loneliness, and yes, grief.

Many are grieving the life they had pre-COVID-19, some are grieving their freedom, and many are grieving their sense of security and normalcy; however, I was stunned to hear how many believe that coupled with their behavioral health issues, and before COVID-19 became a household word, they had the virus. Most believed that the solution would be an antibody test. Why? How might it help if you did have access to an antibody test which resulted in a positive result? Many tell me that a positive antibody test would change their perspective – their sense of freedom and security may be rejuvenated. They may have the ability to help others with the research on convalescent plasma from recovered individuals. Most of all, their anxiety and depression would sharply decrease and their "whole outlook would change from a negative to a positive."

One woman expressed that "I would finally be able to sleep, eat, and perhaps even shower. I have been numb and unable to motivate myself to do anything!" Another stated, "I feel like I'm in a box, powerless. Every time I hear the press conference with more or longer restrictions, the box gets smaller. Pretty soon I'm going to disappear!" "I might be able to breathe again," sobbed another. And still another argues, "Many say the virus was around in November, so wouldn't it be great to find out that it was COVID-19, and one may be immune!"

Hundreds of individuals have called with some variation of the following story: "I had a really bad flu in (anytime within the months of November to February). I had high fevers, a cough that sounded like I was a barking dog, exhaustion after a four-to-six-hour nap. Even my hair hurt! I went to the doctor, who did a test that revealed I was positive for Influenza A. He/she gave me Tamiflu, cough medicine, and recommended rest and liquids. A week later I was still ill. I went back to the doctor who concluded I had 'secondary complications to the flu' and gave me a Z-Pak. Weeks later and I still wasn't back to normal! I had a flu shot, but I still got a horrible flu. What if it was Corona before they knew about it? We all thought China was some place far away that would never affect me. In fact, when I left the doctor, he chuckled and said, 'You'll be fine! Just don't go to China!'"

I am unsure whether we are looking at the antibody test as a treatment to assuage anxiety, depression, loneliness, or grief. But for those hundreds of people who have called us, fraught with behavioral health issues, their hopes for sanity is hanging in the balance as they pray for a positive antibody test. I was compelled to address the elephant in the room: "What if the antibody test is negative?" Most responded similarly: "Well, at least I'd know. I'd have to accept the inevitable. BUT if it's positive I will be free. The not knowing is the hardest part."

A Personal Reflection on Surviving "Stay at Home" Orders

Choices

I have heard this pandemic compared to several Stephen King novels, or *The Hunger Games*, *Divergent*, and for the older folks, an episode of "*The Twilight Zone*." At the outset, everyone scrambled for necessities and followed every edict heard, both nationally and locally. It seems like we have only recently come out of our stupor and have begun to take stock in our own views and not follow like a herd of supplicant sheep. We (or I) recognized we still have choices.

Since my childhood, my family has referred to me as "Mari quite contrary," and perhaps that moniker was appropriate then, but now I see it as a passionate fire to take control of my life as I see fit. Pre-COVID-19, I was teaching in a classroom, seeing clients in my office, and volunteering for Teen Challenge Rhode Island and the American Red Cross. I was swimming about a mile every day at my local gym and bringing my dogs to the dog park.

When the virus attacked, I, like many, experienced a modicum of fear, surrealism, and panic; however, when I traveled to Florida in early January, I wore a mask – despite the cry not to wear one. I began to come out of the COVID-19 vacuum to use my common sense. Since then, I have made modifications in my lifestyle that make this existence more palatable. I remembered and reminded myself again: I have a choice. We all have choices.

1. After the first two weeks of wearing sweats, I woke up and gave myself a good talking to. "Mari, you are not helpless; this situation will not get you." Since that renewed epiphany…

2. I choose to have my meals on my favorite china and crystal, marking each meal as an event.

3. I chose to purchase a bicycle. Riding has changed my outlook dramatically, with lots of vitamins and fresh air along with a feeling of freedom.

4. I chose to purchase hundreds of perennials as a reminder. When they bloom it will be a sign.

5. I chose to purchase bags of small pieces of tile to decorate the top of a tree stump, making it look like the tabletop from a small café in Naples, Italy.

6. I chose to purchase a difficult and challenging paint by number.

7. I live near the beach. When the governor closed the beaches and the dog parks, I walked there. I took the dogs and ran along the shoreline or walked the wall at Narragansett, always with face covering and gloves.

8. On good weather days, I choose to put my convertible top down and drive as far as I can, with the wind in my hair, my favorite tunes blasting on the radio, always accompanied by one of the dogs in my passenger seat.

9. My biggest hurdle was to imitate my near-daily swims. After careful consideration and research, I chose to purchase a wet suit. Now I can go back to my laps, either in a private pool or the ocean.

10. I choose not to watch the news on a regular basis. It is time-consuming, sucks you into the politics and death totals, and can result in 24 hours of rumination and perseveration. Less is better.

11. I choose to take a long, hot bath at day's end.

When we get caught up in both the minutiae and the significance of the impact of this pandemic, we risk becoming myopic. We are intelligent, adept human beings who want to empower ourselves and be empowered by others. I for one do not want to be enabled. We can recognize and make choices, albeit limited at this time, but choices nonetheless. We simply need a bit of ingenuity and creativity and the ability to be independent, passionate, and maybe a bit "contrary."

Corona Virus and the Grievers

A new client, Sharon, came into my office yesterday. When she checked off "always" for "lonely" on the intake assessment, I noted this and brought it up later in the session. "What does lonely feel like for you? What emotions do you associate with loneliness?" "Sad," she replied. "Sad and lonely because my adult daughter died, and lonely because she's gone."

Sharon represents the thousands of grievers across the world who feel alone, lonely, and sad. These expected reactions to acute grief (the first six months after the death) are exacerbated exponentially by the new normal of social distancing. I heartily agree with Kindred Psychology's Facebook post "Let's reframe Social Distancing and call it Physical Distancing and Social Solidarity Movement. We need each other."

Isn't that what we really mean? Physical distancing? Semantics matter. The prevalence of this coronavirus has resulted in an increase of mental health issues of depression and anxiety. And loneliness. We need to physically distance ourselves from the grievers, along with hospitalized patients and loved ones in nursing homes and assisted living facilities. They are all lonely, but our grievers experience a different kind of lonely, perhaps combined with depression and anxiety along with physical and psychological pain. Be empathetic. Put yourself in their place. Have you ever grieved? Then picture yourself at that moment with a mandate to hunker down at home.

Moreover, funeral homes and churches are mandated to follow the physical distancing protocol. This means that you can have no more than 25 people in the funeral home at one time, despite several wakes occurring simultaneously. Masses have been cancelled; however, you may have a brief service (no Mass, no communion) with no more than 25 grievers. We cannot conduct a celebration of life or the closure that wakes and funerals provide. This is the new (temporary) normal.

As we reach out to those in need — the elderly, disabled, children, pregnant mothers and nursing babies — we need to reach out to the grievers. Call. FaceTime. Send a virtual card, a kind email. There are also online chat rooms for grievers. Don't forget them. Let's engage in a social solidarity movement. We all need each other.

The Gift of Goodbye

"We long for the gift of goodbye…
Where do we go from here?
The sadness won't just disappear
Watching the clock it never stops
Where do we go from here?"
(Lyrics by Joe Matira/Dean Petrella, July 2020)

'Tis the season. Children have crafted their wish lists for Santa, families and friends play "Secret Santa" along with many a Facebook post that encourage us to join a virtual chain-letter-type gift-giving list to strangers. Perhaps to just make this particular season a bit brighter.

In an effort to maintain a semblance of reality and control, many families have their Christmas trees displayed by Thanksgiving, along with outdoor lights and holiday decorations in their yards. Windows display white candles, and front doors are dressed in extravagant wreaths. We all love this season. We all want this season. We all need this season.

There is a flurry of delivery trucks following black Monday, with many a doorstep crowded with boxes that display the Amazon logo. We love to give. This year we have a bit more time to ponder the perfect gift for our parents, children, brothers, and sisters.

What's on your wish list?

My clients have only one gift request. One that in former years would have been possible. Simple. Not this year. Not 2020.

"All I want for Christmas is the gift of goodbye."

No amount of money or prayers can fulfill their wishes. Their parents die in nursing homes, hospital beds, hospice, assisted living. These settings are closed to visitors. Due to COVID.

Diane can wave to her grandmother from a window. A woman who raised her and had the greatest impact on who she is today. Paula and Kathy's mom is in a nursing home with hospice care. Kiel's daughter was in a horrific car accident, but he cannot sit by her side as she struggles for each breath.

Liam is on life support following an accidental overdose. He is alone when the medical team determines that he is brain dead and sends in the transplant team to harvest his organs. No one knew he had checked off organ donor on his driver's license.

Oh sure, we have FaceTime. A technological appeasement that cannot replace human presence. Most will die alone, without the human touch of hand over hand, without the stroking of their hair, without a kiss or a hug. Dying alone is often reported by human beings as their biggest fear.

Following the death, we face more restrictions. Limited visitation at the funeral home. Limited presence at the church/mosque/synagogue.

"Can we just stand outside their gravesite and have a small memorial service?" No.

We grieve for ourselves, for the interrupted life, like immersing ourselves in a sizeable novel only to find the last page had been ripped out.

Allow me to ask a rhetorical question. Is this fair or unfair? Given the risk of COVID do you respect the edicts to "stay away?" Or, would you rather take a risk for that one and only gift you require?

The gift of goodbye.

Part 3

Trauma

TEN STORIES

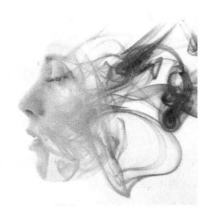

The Masks in the Room

Don't be fooled by me.
Don't be fooled by the face I wear
For I wear a mask, a thousand masks,
Masks that I am afraid to take off, and none of them is me...
Beneath lies confusion, and fear, and
Aloneness...
That's why I frantically create a mask to hide behind...
To help me pretend,
To shield the glance that knows.
I tell you everything that's really nothing,
And nothing of what's everything,
Of what's crying within me...
Please listen carefully and try to hear what I'm not saying...
Who am I, you may wonder?
I am someone you know very well.
For I am every man you meet
And I am every woman you meet.
[Who wears a mask}
(Excerpts from "Please Hear What I'm Not Saying" Charles C. Finn)

The history of masks dates back to 7000 BC, where they were used for rituals and ceremonies. As centuries passed, the use of masks grew to include the need for protection, disguise, and entertainment.

In 1966, Charles C. Finn could not possibly have envisioned a world where everyone is mandated to don a literal mask; he was referring to a metaphorical, symbolic mask. Masks that we all wear to control how people perceive us, often referred to by sociologists as the "looking-glass self."

These masks can be interchangeable, and require a great deal of emotional energy and vigilance to wear and change, sometimes in seconds. Yet, Finn says we all wear masks. Those of us who are adept but exhausted from wearing them may be relieved that we can wear a tangible mask; one that covers the metaphorical one and reduces emotional hiding.

In 2020 we all wear a mask that makes it easier for us to hide, and more difficult for others to read our facial expressions. This mask policy interferes with counseling/therapy because we normally "hear" what a person is not saying through their body language, which includes facial expressions. Social psychologists discuss the importance of body language, as it represents about 56% of what we truly communicate. In fact, the words we use reflect only 7% of what we are genuinely feeling. The remainder, 37%, is attributed to tone, rate, and volume of speech. Think about this: if body language is 56%, it is apparent that we need to listen with our eyes, as we watch what someone's words are trying to hide or manipulate. It's very difficult to "fake" or manipulate one's body language – our words can lie but body language cannot (unless of course one is a seasoned actor or performer). They can lie with body language as well.

We do, however, have an advantage with our literal masks, as our eyes are more pronounced, more prevalent, and considered the "windows of the soul." Yet without the benefit of the entire facial expression, we may inaccurately identify the subtext ("actions speak louder than words," "don't listen to what people say, watch what they do"). This inability to see a three-dimensional face is the fuel for misunderstanding both the message and the emotion.

But then again, perhaps a person's choice of mask is revealing. Some include memes, quotes from favorite Netflix series, others reflect a sports team or a Broadway show. Maybe these literal masks reveal more than what we might learn otherwise. For some.

Personally, I am grieving over the loss of faces, their form, their skin color (are they blushing, are they angry?). This grief is founded on years of hearing subtexts through my eyes, analyzing and interpreting when a client doesn't even know their facial expressions and body movements belie their words. Now, it is difficult to assess the emotional state because I know their words are only 7% reliable. One needs to hear and see the contradictions. Are they clenching their jaw under that Patriots mask? Are their lips trembling under the *Schitt's Creek* mask, even though their words indicate they are happy? My failsafe is their tone, rate, and volume of speech. A whisper is equally as telling as a wail. The mask mandate has forced the professional in me to work harder, attune myself more to the speaker, increase my empathic skills, and share their space.

I am also charged with teaching graduate students how to do the same, as they struggle to perfect their listening and therapeutic skills. I emphasize to my soon-to-be therapist students that my default, and theirs as well, is authenticity. Genuineness. This may bypass the problems of communication – if we can have congruency in our words, body language, and tone/rate/volume. We are models for our clients, and our sessions are a microcosm of their lives. By encouraging authenticity and congruency/consistency we can facilitate the growth and change in our clients. Even with masks.

Students often refer to my incessant quote, "Address the elephant in the room." We all have unsaid or unthought issues. We all have an elephant behind our mask. Finn's poem discusses the lengths to which we go to hide who we really are, our vulnerabilities, and our Achille's heel(s). If we share what we are thinking or feeling we will not be distracted with the busyness of the layers, bundles, and threads of thoughts in our mind.

Maybe, just maybe, masks can help us reveal. And through reveal we heal.

Technology in Death and Grief

The fact that technology is ubiquitous can present both advantages and disadvantages in the field of thanatology (the study of death and dying).

Take Diana, a single mom of three teenage sons. The boys, Jack, Jim, and Jacob were each two years apart. They were a very tight-knit family as Diana felt she needed to be both mom and dad to her boys. She became a den mother when her boys wanted to join the Boy Scouts, served as a teaching assistant in their grammar school, and chaperoned their school field trips. The boys were all athletic and one could always find Diana in the stands for every basketball, baseball, and football game. The boys were each other's best friends, and they all shared the same friends. Diana's home was always the favorite destination of all the boys in the neighborhood, who would land there after school or a game. It wasn't unusual for Diana to cook for eight to ten hungry boys, or host weekend sleepovers where pup tents were set up in her backyard. She didn't have much money, but she made up for it with love.

As they grew older, she joined both their middle and high school PTOs and was a familiar presence in the halls as a library aide. After a Friday night basketball game, Jacob texted Diana to inform her that he and his brothers, along with another friend, Garrett, were going to grab some food at the local pub on Curry Street. She told Jacob to be safe, have fun, and text before they left the restaurant. Two hours later she received the expected text from Jacob. "Heading home, just going to drop Garrett off at his house. Love you." All was well.

It was a bit unusual for Diana to be home alone. In order to entertain herself while waiting for her boys, she watched Netflix while she absently scrolled through Facebook.

A moment later, she froze. She stopped scrolling at a picture that had been posted five minutes prior. It was the scene of a horrific car accident. Police, fire and rescue were at the scene and someone had posted "terrible accident on Curry, watching as they use jaws of life. Looks like at least two dead. Car hit a tree head on."

Diana learned of the death of Jacob, who was driving, and Jim, who was in the front passenger seat, through social media. Jack and Garrett had been sitting in the backseat and Diana soon learned that they were both in critical condition. When the police arrived, Diana knew the story. Home alone, waiting for her three boys who did not return. According to the police, two were at the state morgue and the other in ICU. (Both did survive).

Diana's story is not unique; many family members learn of horrific accidents and deaths through Facebook, posted by seemingly naïve individuals attempting to get the word out. This is a cautionary tale – I strongly urge you to avoid posting any grisly scenes or posts that announce a death on any social media platforms. It is information you cannot take back and may cause a traumatic grief reaction.

In the recent past there has also been a plethora of examples where individuals have sent "suicide texts" rather than leaving a note. Take Samantha. A 26-year-old newly married (two years) woman who had just given birth to a beautiful, healthy, baby boy. At just three months old, her son still required a great deal of time, and her husband Nathan often pitched in. One early fall evening, Samantha called Nathan from downstairs for his help with a broken kitchen faucet. Nathan shouted back, "I'm running out to the store to get some milk. Be back in ten," and with that he walked out the front door.

Approximately seven minutes later, Samantha received a text from Nathan. "I love you. You and our son are the two most important people in my life. I'm so sorry. Please forgive me." Samantha's heart began to pound. What did Nathan mean? Why was he sorry?

Nathan never made it to the store. He suicided by gun shortly after sending the text.

The above are two tragic stories that are replicated daily with the ubiquity of technology; however, there are some advantages. Memorial Facebook pages are created for the deceased where people can post messages days, months, and even years later. They can reminisce as if they were perusing an old photo album.

Some of my clients save texts or voice mails from the deceased loved one to listen or read them over and over. There is some controversy over the efficacy of this; however, a client of mine whose boyfriend accidently overdosed on fentanyl stated that her ability to listen to his voicemail and text his phone with messages as to how much she misses him has made her grieving more manageable. She feels it maintains their connection.

Technology can be both detrimental or advantageous in death and grief. Please stop and think before you post and maintain connections when they prove therapeutic.

Death and Non-death Losses

There is grief associated with both death and non-death losses.

They have been sexually abused as children, trafficked as adolescents and adults, jailed, homeless, living on the streets and compromised their self-worth through prostitution, stealing and neglecting their children. Regina was sexually abused by her father at age eleven, Donna's father shot her up at age ten. She lived in a storage unit for two years and has three children in foster care. They will all tell you that they thought this was normal living. Addicted, with negligent parents, Susan was raped at age sixteen. The women have lost loved ones, their identities, their virginity, their children, and their childhoods to active addiction. All these girls turned to drugs as a coping mechanism for the horrors they endured and the losses they experienced to opioid deaths. Yes, some became addicted to opiates from a surgery or injury, some to peer pressure despite a loving home, but they are all addicts. More importantly, they are all addicts in recovery. You can see the before and after pictures on their websites and Facebook pages. You'll understand.

I know their stories well. I am a clinical volunteer at Teen Challenge Rhode Island, and I've sat with them once a week for the past two years. This is where these girls live for 15 months, where thousands of broken women have come and successfully graduated for the past 25 years. The unassuming building on 572 Elmwood Avenue belies the miracles that occur behind these modest doors. Of course, there is pain, hurt, guilt, and shame, and a grief that is tangible. It's not emotional baggage they carry, but rather "griefcases." Without the drugs, they have no eraser. Every emotion, interaction and behavior are new. They are like newborns in sobriety.

Deborah Manzo McDonald is the director of TCRI and has been since the doors first opened 25 years ago. She and her staff "love the residents back to life;" however, the irony is apparent. Deborah lost her son, a prominent Connecticut attorney, to an accidental overdose just three years ago. How does one save all these women yet is unable to save her own son? Her grief manifests itself differently than most people. Of course, she has experienced the numbing, surreal, heartbreak of the loss of her first- born son. She has been unable to stop her tears or leave her room. She has sat with photo albums of JoJo for hours on end. It's been three years and she still has trouble believing he is gone. Yet Deborah has a strong faith and an abiding love for God. She has put her grief in His hands and asked Him to direct her through a life without her son.

I shared a telling story with Deborah, about a man who lost his 18-year-old daughter. At the cemetery the minister asked the man, "If God said to you at your daughter's birth, 'I'm giving you this precious baby girl, but I will need to take her back in 18 years, would you still want her?' The man sobbed and responded yes."

As did Deborah and I expect many of you as well. We grieve for ourselves, for what we have lost: a child, a parent, a childhood, our innocence.

Angel Babies

Grieving the Child You Never Knew

October is Pregnancy and Infant Loss Awareness month. Suzanne had a miscarriage (stillbirth) five months into her first pregnancy, Gretchen gave birth to a stillborn, and Angela had a late-term elective abortion. They are all baby-loss survivors. And in some cases, they are all considered to be "mothers."

Many who have lost a baby that they will never know will experience both ambiguous and disenfranchised grief. Ambiguous loss is one that happens without closure or understanding, where disenfranchised grief is one that is not normally recognized by society. Suzanne experienced a loss without closure as well as a loss not recognized by society. Miscarriages are often considered commonplace and "for the best as the fetus wasn't viable," or "don't worry you can always have more." The impact of a miscarriage can be devastating and result in anger towards others who have had successful pregnancies. About 10-20% of pregnancies result in miscarriage.

With a pregnancy, there exists the excitement over a new role and a new member to welcome into the world. Suzanne had a gender-reveal party and miscarried days after it was revealed she was having a boy. She had already chosen the name Quinn. When she miscarried Quinn, she grieved the little boy she pictured in her mind's eye. Fortunately, many hospitals have created opportunities for closure to minimize ambiguous grief. Nurses provide swaddling clothes or an outfit, allow the parents to cradle the child and memorialize the moments in a family photograph. They may also provide an inked handprint or footprint. I've spoken to several people who believe this ritual is bizarre, as the child is dead; however, eventually they will be a very grateful family. They may choose to have a funeral and a gravesite, or a cremation and keep the ashes of what would have been.

Gretchen is most likely to experience ambiguous loss as society reacts more profoundly and recognizes the depth of grief of losing a stillborn. Gretchen's friends surprised her with an early baby shower, as she had been trying to get pregnant for a long time. The baby's room was decorated, the crib was in place, and a bookcase full of storied treasures waited for the new arrival. The only thing missing was her daughter. She named her Nora. According to the website americanpregnancy.org, "stillbirth is one of the most devasting losses, affecting over 25,000 families each year, most occurring in a problem-free pregnancy."

Like Angela, abortions are often kept secret, which exacerbates the grief and loss exponentially. It is often referred to as the "unspoken loss." What gets obscured is that often abortion is a difficult emotional choice. Some of you may ask, "Why grieve over a loss that was a choice?" Many experience shame and guilt. Abortion, "like every pregnancy, has an individual context and a ...personal meaning." (Kim Kluger-Bell, 1998) According to the CDC, there were 45.7 million abortions in the US between 1970-2015. The fact that it is a choice does not make the pain less bearable. I hear client stories where they dream about the aborted fetus, and, like miscarriages, have given the aborted fetus a name, an identity, so that they can grieve. Many will have long-delayed emotional reaction to an abortion and thus must find a different method of closure.

For any angel baby loss, we need to provide tangible suggestions moving forward. In her book entitled *Unspeakable Losses: Healing from Miscarriage, Abortion and Other Pregnancy Loss*, Kluger-Bell offers suggestions which include:

1. Don't inadvertently minimize the emotional impact of early losses and abortions.

2. Offer and encourage parent(s) to touch, hold, and/or photograph the fetus.

3. Offer supportive resources, i.e. designing ceremonies and memorials.

4. Prepare yourself for misdirected rage. Try to stay emotionally available and be willing to listen.

5. Encourage the parent(s) to give themselves plenty of time to recover and resist the impulse to try and "fix" their emotional distress.

6. Guilt and shame may play a huge role in preventing people from working through their grief.

If you find yourself in need of a safe space to cope, I encourage you to research available, unbiased resources like "Exhale" (exhaleprovoice.org), a hotline and website for women post-abortion and a great book entitled *The Healing Choice: Your Guide to Emotional Recovery after an Abortion* by Candace du Puy and Dana Dovitch. There is also a website called the Miscarriage Association (www.miscarriageassociation.org.uk) and "Emotional support after miscarriage" (www.pregnancybirth-baby.org.au). Cathy Blanford's book *Something Happened* is a book for children and adults who have experienced a pregnancy loss.

Allow me to leave you with a quote by Angela Miller as we recognize Pregnancy and Infant Loss Awareness Month:

> "My child died.
> I don't need advice.
> All I need is for you
> To gently close your mouth,
> Open wide your heart and
> Walk with me until
> I can see color again."

American Red Cross
Second Responders Needed

Rosa, an elderly woman, always accompanied by her walker and oxygen tank, left a pot on the stove and took a little nap.

The family of seven, who declined help to install smoke alarms, missed the symptomatic evidence and never smelled the smoke.

A city was ravaged by floods and its residents were powerless to save their property.

These are only a few examples of our clients at the American Red Cross, Territory 6. T6 serves people of Rhode Island and Seekonk, Massachusetts.

We are second responders, called in by first responders when people have been displaced due to a disaster. Big or small, we offer comfort, compassion, and financial support to people who have experienced the loss of their homes. Family photos, objects valuable only to them, everything they have worked for is now gone. This displacement is a non-finite loss, and those affected grieve this loss.

I am a volunteer with T6. The varied amount of areas for volunteerism is extraordinary – I serve on both the DAT and the ICCT teams. DAT is the Disaster Action Team, who responds to local disasters or can be deployed to long-term displacement by setting up shelters. ICCT is an acronym for Integrated Care and Condolence Team. We respond to people who have experienced a loss of a family member (Sandy Hook) or a missing person.

About 90% of the American Red Cross is comprised of volunteers. We respond to any disaster when contacted by police, fire, and rescue. The position of a Red Cross volunteer is both rewarding and humbling. People are scared, anxious, and lost.

"What about my medication?" "My bible is still in the apartment; can you go in and get it for me?" "I don't have any food." "Where will I sleep?" "I don't have any clothes and it's freezing outside."

We arrive in our Red Cross van with blankets, snacks, and water as we assure them that we are there to help them. We supply financial support for a hotel room, call appropriate contacts to get them their medication, and supply donated items. The physical and psychological needs are addressed on site even before people are transferred to a warm space.

In both local and national disasters, we set up shelters with volunteers who serve as clerical, intake, case managers, mental health workers, and cooks. We work with local agencies to provide what has been lost and identify needed services. We also provide pet shelters for long-term displacement and create activities for children in the shelter. We also have an international Disaster Action Team for those who prefer to respond to disasters overseas.

Whatever first responders identify as needs, we are there for them. There is no cost to volunteer. All travel and meals and lodging are provided by the Red Cross. Any time is a good time to volunteer, but as we are on the cusp of 2020, I invite you to consider this opportunity. Giving of ourselves is a rich experience. Please join me in helping people survive these devasting losses.

You will sleep well.

The American Red Cross, Rhode Island Chapter (T6) office is located at 100 Niantic Avenue, Suite A, in Providence, Rhode Island. The phone number is 401-831-7700. Phil Stocking is the Senior Director of Disaster Cycle Services, T6.

I thank you.

Dirty Laundry

I often ask my clients to journal for homework. The following is 45-year-old Thomasina's journal entry about her rape and the first and only time she told the story. Ironically, she chose to share her story with men incarcerated in a men's maximum-security prison. She was a high school English teacher.

"They called me Miss T, as inmates are not privy to our last names. They sat discussing the pros and cons of committing rape versus murder. I was facilitating a bibliotherapy group in a men's maximum-security prison. Today's story was Mary Gordon's short story "Violation," in which the female narrator begins by saying, 'I suppose that in a forty-five-year life, I should be grateful to have experienced only two instances of sexual molestation.'" (page 397)

Ralph Cosgrove agreed. A tall, lanky, well-read and literate forty-something-year-old with a military crew cut was serving a 30-year sentence for the rape of his 13-year-old developmentally delayed daughter.

"Miss T, you have to admit that she really was grateful; the life she describes is so boring and mundane that she was indeed appreciative of the rapes. They serve as the highlights; the only exciting experiences she had in her drab, little, pitiful, traditional life."

"Cosgrove, you are so screwed up! Sorry, Miss T, you are crazy! She was being sarcastic! She didn't really mean she liked the rapes – they weren't exciting!" Ray Barrino argued.

Ralph, who always spoke in a monotone cadence, replied calmly and solicitously, "Barrino, I suggest you re-read her description of the rape in Ireland… Never mind, I'll read it to all of you." Ralph referred to a page and began, 'In conclusion, she didn't resist. She never said no. Which means she liked it.'" Ralph looked up at the group, making silent eye contact with each one of them.

Julio Martinez, who had remained silent, spoke up, as usual, gritting his teeth to ameliorate his anger. "Cosgrove – you skipped somethin'."

"By all means, Martinez," Cosgrove replied, with a palm-up hand sweep invitation theatrical bow. "Please, enlighten us."

Julio, whose spoken English was second only to his reading the language, began to stumble over the words as he read. "'I did as he said, closed my eyes. I didn't want to look at him AND…I don't know when I realized that I was in danger…' So there, she says so herself. She was scared."

Julio continued, addressing the rest of the 11 members of the group. "You guys know why I'm here. Triple homicide, which makes me a serial killer. Lifer. No parole. But I'll tell all of yous, I would kill anyone, any time before I would RAPE 'em! That's all I got to say, Miss. T."

Julio's statement was met with many nods, a few high-fives and a "Damn straight, Martinez" from Tommy Fung. Outnumbered, Ralph showed no emotion as he replied, "Martinez, Barrino, Fung, allow me a moment to clarify your views. Am I correct in assuming that you all feel that taking someone's life is more acceptable than simply raping them?"

This time Tommy Fung stood up and angrily banged his fist against the wall, shouting, "Damn straight, Cosgrove! When you kill someone, their life is over! When you rape someone, you let them live when they are all screwed up and have mental problems."

Cosgrove staunchly replied, "You are highly mistaken, Fung. Rape leaves the victims with a choice as to how they want to live the remainder of their lives. They might choose to simply forget about it. Murder is final. We have no right to take a life. No one does, except God. Perhaps we should survey rape victims and ask if they would rather be dead."

I asked myself, *Should I tell them?*

It was a balmy postcard evening in the Bahamas, the last evening of our senior high school class trip. Fifteen 17-year-old girls from a private, Catholic high school were celebrating at a small, local club called The Hot Spot. Randy was a 25-year-old white, native islander with an Afro: funky, cool, and manager of the night's band. He was the kind of guy every girl wanted. He wanted me. He approached me to ask for the last dance. Despite the heat, Randy wore a black leather jacket that bled sweat as we danced. As the last chord played, the house lights went up, indicating closing time. I was aware that Randy still had his arm around my waist as he began to shout commands at the roadies from the band. "Hey, what did you say your name was?" Randy asked in a low, soft, cool voice with a tinge of a British accent.

"I didn't. It's Thomasina."

"Great name, Thomasina. I'm gonna call you Tommy. Listen Tommy, I am really, really attracted to you. Let's spend some more time together." I told him we were flying out the next morning. "Well, that sucks," he said. "Hey, how about taking a walk back to my place for a cupper? You know, true island style?" I looked around the deserted club. There was no sign of any of my classmates, although our hotel was just around the corner. "Sure," I replied. "How far is it?"

"Oh sunshine, it's just a short walk on a full moon. Hang on, let me grab my keys." We walked in silence until we reached a three-story tenement. "That's my place – top floor. If you look out the window and squint, you can see the water and your hotel. Wait 'til I grab a flashlight; these lights can be a bitch in the dark. Wouldn't want Tommy Sunshine to fall and get hurt." Randy crouched down under the first step and took out the flashlight that was hidden in the dirt.

As he unlocked the front door, I chose not to notice the chipped paint, the drab old wallpaper, or the single lightbulb that hung over the second-floor landing. I was excited, curious, and flattered. I thought, this is going to be a great story to tell my friends! We entered a very small, one room, cramped, half-dormered space. Against the wall to the right was a bed that appeared to be a pull-out couch. It was stained and smelled of mold, and the wooden headboard indicated an old, ornate mahogany. Plaid couch cushions were strewn all over the floor and the three-legged, scratched coffee table sat where an end table should be, its fourth side held up by a stack of magazines. The top magazine peeked out of the stack. It was pornography. I hate pornography.

"Sorry there is nowhere to sit, Tommy Sunshine. Just sit on the corner of the bed. Forgot to make it." Randy seemed to disappear around the corner into what I could only guess was the kitchen.

As I waited, I wondered what time it was. Not because I was in a hurry but because I wanted time to stop. I heard the teapot whistle and Randy shouted, "Be out in a sec." I waited to hear the creak of the black leather jacket as a signal that he was finally returning. But all was silent.

I was stunned when he emerged from the kitchen. He held a beautiful, ornate silver tray that balanced two matching teacups, each decorated with mauve roses in bloom, outlined with gold trim and coupled with a matching sugar and creamer and two hand-embroidered lace cotton napkins. Randy was completely naked.

I had never seen a naked man before. I panicked. "What's going on?" I asked Randy. "Why are you naked?" I was very confused and honestly did not understand. I was mesmerized by the tea set. It reminded me of the miniature tea set that Mama B gave my twin sister Francesca and me on our fifth birthday, so we could serve a proper tea to our dolls.

"C'mon on, sunshine. Did you really think I invited you back just for tea?!"

I sat stupidly as he placed the tray on the three-legged coffee table and turned toward me. "C'mon, sunshine. God, you're beautiful. Let me feel you." He leaned in over me, bracing himself with his flat palms on the corner of the mattress. I began to get nervous. "No, Randy, I mean, yes, I did think we were just going to have tea. I think there has been a mistake."

"No mistake, Thomasina, you c--t. You American girls are alike." He then let his hands go and fell on top of me with his full weight. As I squirmed to get out from under him, he put his hands under my shoulders and lifted me so that my head was now at the top of the bed. "C'mon, Tommy Sunshine, let me have you. Easy or hard, I will have you."

I kept my eyes on the tea set and went from a whisper to a scream. "No, Randy, no. Please let me go. My friends will be looking for me and the chaperone will be calling the police!"

"Nice try, you little American hottie." He lifted my head and held it in both hands as he began to bang my head against the wooden mahogany headboard. It hurt. With every bang he muttered "F---in' American whore." Bang. "American tease." Bang. Harder and faster. "F---ing American c---s." I kept my eyes on the tea set, thinking that Mama B would be disappointed that Randy hadn't thought to include the little frosted tea cakes.

Then everything went black.

It was daylight when I opened my eyes. I was alone, still on my back on the bed. A slight sliver of sunlight cut through a torn window shade and illuminated the blood. My dress had been ripped down the middle, my sheer white tights in shreds, while blood pooled between my legs and crusted on my inner thighs. I felt dizzy and nauseous as I tried to raise my head. The last thing I remembered was the tea set, which remained on the coffee table, the tea now cold.

I had to get out of that place. I struggled to get up and heard a chuckle. I looked up to see a still naked Randy, his head cocked to one side as he drew in a long, languid, drag from his cigarette. "Morning, Tommy Sunshine," he laughed. I tied up my dress as best I could. He didn't move when I stumbled out of the door. When I finally reached the bottom of the stairs I limped into full sunlight, still hearing his chuckle. As I rounded the corner of the yard near the side of his house I saw him. He posed, naked on the top step of the fire escape, still watching, still smoking.

As I finally entered the hotel lobby, our chaperone was pacing, speaking with the hotel concierge. She took one look at me and cried, running up to me and repeating, "Where have you been? What happened to you?" I didn't know that my face was covered in blood and bruises.

"It was my moped, Mrs. Jackson! It was dark, and I forgot about driving on the opposite side of the road. A car was coming so I swerved and hit a stone wall. I guess I have a concussion, because I blacked out and don't remember anything!"

She bought it. I flew home with a story I would not tell. Until now.

My story was met with stone silence. "What happened?" asked Julio. "I don't know," I responded.

"Miss T, why all the blood?" asked Fung.

"Because I was a virgin. I was naïve, immature, and stupid."

"Why didn't you tell anyone?" asked Barrino.

"I thought it was my fault."

Cosgrove cleared his throat and asked, "Well Miss T, would you rather be dead?"

Most times, I thought.

The Peace Monument, Turkey

This is My Brave

I am no stranger to protests. The recent ones associated with Black Lives Matter have brought back memories that I feel compelled to share with you today. Sometimes memories lay dormant, but these memories are now alive and well, having been given a voice and a new breath by the horror of George Floyd's murder and the subsequent violence. I know violence as well, through the eyes of those that have suffered at another time. In another place. Allow my indulgence as writing the moments deflates the emotional intensity of the memories.

My first protest was in 1970, the Women's Strike for Equality. Subsequent participation included 1972/1973, first in Florida and again in San Francisco, when we marched in the "Take Back the Night" protest in an effort to demand resources and safety for all women and against violent snuff pornography films. Another was in 1975, as a student in a small, all-female, Catholic college. We wanted to rid ourselves of the president of our institution for "no confidence." One can still find a copy of the Brookline Chronicle where I am in full view on the front page, in a sit-in on the front lawn of the administration building. The 1970s and early 1980s were my years of anger and righteous indignation. I marched for women's rights, against war, for LGBT rights, and for the AIDS project.

The Kent State shootings in 1970 took place during a peace rally against the Vietnam War. I was already a warrior and a feminist by the time the Kent State massacre occurred. I had a dog named Libby (short for Women's Liberation Movement), had burned my bra (despite reports that it never happened – it was simply symbolic), and had taken on the persona of a stereotypical, quintessential hippie. PEACE and LOVE.

For me, it was the Kent State shooting that fueled my fear and the communal passion of college students all over the Unites States. We were peaceful protesters. They were killed. This could have been us.

> "Tin soldiers and Nixon's coming
> We're finally on our own.
> This summer I hear the drumming
> Four dead in Ohio" (Neil Young, "Ohio," 1970)

It was the draft that caused the rise in our collective ire as we watched birthdates drawn, not unlike the lottery numbers announced on the evening news today. It was scary and I often felt as if I was the one getting stoned in Shirley Jackson's short story, "The Lottery."

"Is it my brother's birthdate?"

"Is it my boyfriend's birthdate?"

"Is it my best friend's birthdate?"

In 1971 I attended the May Day Protests in Washington D.C. — 35,000 strong, we protested against the United States involvement in the Vietnam War. Along with three of my college roommates, we missed finals and hitchhiked from Boston, Massachusetts, to Washington, D.C., each in traditional hippie garb: barefoot, ripped jeans, Wallace Beery shirts, and long, Rastafarian-like hair. We sat in the sun in West Potomac Park near the Washington Monument, as we listened to the likes of Carole King and James Taylor. By day's end, 12,000 were arrested. We were bold. We were passionate. We were 19 years old.

Many friends and loved ones went to Canada to avoid the draft. Some burned their draft cards. Others went off to war and still others went off to college. A college deferment was a guarantee you would live to see another day.

In hindsight, draft dodgers were granted immunity under President Carter, there was an uptick in college degrees, and those who survived the war came home not to a celebratory parade as in other wars, but to be spit upon along with disparaging remarks, criticism, and blame.

Several decades later I met a young Cambodian man who, with his family, was escorted out of Phnom Penh, Cambodia, by the Khmer Rouge, a communist guerilla organization made up of merciless boys. This young man's father was beheaded by a machete-carrying member of the Khmer Rouge, a disciple of Pol Pot. I asked myself, *Is he one of the people I fought so hard against helping?*

I had the fortune to meet another Cambodian in the late 1980s, a young woman with three children. She was living in Rhode Island with her two sons and a new husband. She was also forced to leave her Cambodian home and walked through the jungles in order to reach Thailand. The following is her account:

"My husband was killed by the Khmer Rouge, beheaded for looking over his shoulder while in line to leave Cambodia. I was left to fend for myself and my three boys. I was walking through the jungle, and at the time, I was breastfeeding my infant. We had no food. I began to breast feed all three of my children; the oldest was five. Soon my milk dried up. I went off into the fields to find some grain or something to eat. The Khmer Rouge found us. I told them we were hungry. The Khmer Rouge did not allow resistance or any sign of emotion. No crying allowed or they would kill us.

"'Oh, you are hungry. Pol Pot would not want you hungry. We will feed you.'

"They took my infant. I could show no fear. They had a small fire pit going. As we watched in horror, they took my infant son and skewered him. Then they put the skewer over the fire and hand-turned it methodically, like a rotisserie, roasting him like a pig.

"We were then forced to eat him. And then allowed to leave unharmed."

It was this story that both saddened and enraged me. I made the decision to DO SOMETHING – move from protesting to actively advocating and volunteering my skills to a variety of culturally diverse groups. As an adult I resolved to contribute and assist disenfranchised populations, working with the homeless, the drug addicted, Vietnam-era war veterans, Cambodian refugees, the mentally ill, children in DCYF (Department of Child, Youth, and Families) custody for CASA (Court

Appointed Special Advocate in the Family Court System), and incarcerated men and women in maximum security.

I went on to produce two documentaries: "Rhode Island Voices on Violence, Perspectives on Peace" and "Cathy's Story," a case study of a young woman whose father shot her up with heroin at age five. Cathy spent the next 20 years addicted, homeless, and a prostitute. Most recently I was awarded a Fulbright specialist scholarship to the University of Zululand in South Africa and experienced up-close and personal the impact of apartheid and the AIDS epidemic, as well as the virgin cleansing cure (the belief that having sex with a virgin girl cures a man of HIV/AIDS).

The sum of these experiences increased my awareness of diversity and provided firsthand knowledge. Experience, awareness, and knowledge = empathy, understanding, and respect.

Currently I share these experiences and encourage my students to do the same. I am still a peace lover, a "make love not war" proponent, and I believe in empowerment rather than enabling. I will continue to provide tools for resilience, communication, and success.

I am not a stranger to protests – nor am I stranger to others' pain. Thank you for indulging me.

Peace out.

Resilience

Resilience. This word is usually defined as "ability to bounce back," "the capacity to recover quickly from difficulties," and/or "toughness." This is an admirable trait that lends itself to a successful life, both psychologically and behaviorally. Do you consider yourself resilient? If so, why? If not, why? The bigger question is, can resilience be learned? Many professionals will answer with a resounding "yes"!

I was recently asked during an interview, "What, if anything, did I learn about myself during the pandemic?"

I replied, "I don't think I learned anything new, but some qualities were reinforced."

One was resilience.

I often wish I had a basketful of resilience to distribute to those who are struggling and stuck in the quicksand of childhood trauma. I am constantly amazed at the amount of trauma, abuse, and the damage people have experienced at a very early age.

It is no wonder they opted for drugs and alcohol. I would be very surprised if they hadn't. What are the alternatives? In their cases, staying alive is equivalent to resilience. Many who experience what these girls have endured have opted for suicide, self-harm, and in severe cases, disassociation. And yet they persevere. This might be the 50th time they have tried to get clean. Relapse is part of recovery. In their case, they pray. And surprisingly. they forgive.

Allow me to introduce three clients I met just this week.

Laura has forgiven her husband, who threw her off a bridge. Despite a nine-week coma, she has also forgiven her boyfriend for hitting her in the back of her head with a hammer while she was taking a shower.

And then there is Prudence. She was raped by her father and eventually took a job where her supervisor, a former military man who specialized in tactical interrogation tactics in Afghanistan, practiced on her for a year and a half, hog-tied and sodomized her once or twice a week. Why didn't she report him? That would be a logical question, except to someone who has been physically and sexually abused by her father and forced to live in a closet for four years until she ran away. She learned as a child to be quiet, not to tell. That message stayed with her for over 50 years.

Finally, there is Constance. She left Puerto Rico for a better life in the United States. Also a victim of childhood sexual abuse, she got involved with drugs, drug dealing, prostitution, and gangs. Her search for the American Dream failed her. When her daughter Elia's first birthday approached, Constance decided to return to Puerto Rico to celebrate with her mom and sisters. She left Elia with her sister, Aurora, for a few hours while Constance went on an errand.

Constance's family were very poor. Dirt poor. When her sister Aurora was given a bottle of Lestoil, she danced in delight. Auntie Aurora took her Lestoil and her niece home. She scrubbed the dirt and the memories out of her kitchen floor with a bucket of the precious Lestoil mixed with water. Auntie Aurora took that mop and repetitively dunked it in the bucket, scrubbed, rinsed, and dunked again. Her son Juan and niece Elia played with toy figures in another room. By the time Aurora finished, she was bathed in sweat and satisfaction. She took a quick shower.

When she returned to the kitchen, she found Elia, head-first, drowned in the bucket. Apparently, she had dropped her toy figure in the water and being a small child, she lost her balance, and fell in.

Today, Constance sees her daughter's death not as a tragedy, but a blessing. Hindsight has offered her a new view – a glimpse into the life of a child whose mother would sell her own soul for heroin, who prostituted and abused. Constance feels as if she saved her daughter from her future. Constance also forgives her sister Aurora for her negligence.

These edited autobiographies represent thousands of others. Does childhood abuse and trauma force one to be more resilient? They certainly find coping mechanisms, yet they don't bounce back, they don't have the capacity to recover from difficulties. But they are tough. No matter what life throws at them, they survive the brick walls, as they choose to climb over them rather than being blocked.

At what cost? you ask.

When one loses their childhood, they grieve in ways that seem appropriate to them at the time. Adulthood and residential treatment offer new and more effective ways to deal with this loss. In order to heal, one must reveal. When they graduate from the treatment program, I'd like to add to that diploma, and hand them a certificate in resilience.

A Stroke of Genius

She said she was grieving due to a loss of words. Not voice. Words. Her name is Rosetta, aptly named after the stone. Whether hieroglyphics or shorthand, the stone "represents a crucial key in the process of encoding information." Rosetta is a stunning 60-year-old woman, although one would never guess her age by her appearance, as she is an old soul with young, porcelain skin unmarked by years of deep thinking, which resulted in many stellar poems and lyrics. She is bilingual, and for many years has been an avid logophile (a lover of words), a bibliophile (lover of books/reading), and a melophile (lover of music).

Rosetta was always a unique girl/woman given that she is an old soul. She seems to carry generations of knowledge and thoughts, similar to Jung's collective unconscious, acquired through her reading and writing. She shared this gift with her students in her English classes in an attempt to impress them with words, with writing, with the beauty of music, and with her demanding philosophy for perfection. "Art does not imitate life. Life does not imitate art." "Life is art, art is life."

She adores the classics, the rich treasure trove of words strung together in a sentence that makes the reader weep in despair or cry in ecstasy. This is her legacy. Her words. Her brilliance in describing the mere mundane with a vocabulary stoked from years of reading.

Until she couldn't.

Rosetta suffered a stroke. She stopped teaching. She lost interest and patience in reading. She hesitated when searching for lyrics. Following a great deal of speech and physical therapy, she began to resemble the Rosetta everyone loved and admired; however, she knew her suffering from aphasia/dysphasia (lack of language/impaired language) is a roadblock that seems permanent. She regained her voice, yet still struggles to find her words.

How often have we heard the phrase "I'm at a loss for words" or "I can't seem to find the right word," as if all words are simply free-floating fireflies in our brain and all we need do is shine a flashlight to identify the right word. The aha moment. Rosetta found her flashlight, but it shines dim as she searches the recesses of her mind for the right word. This search is more like a scavenger hunt for her now.

Rosetta is one of the most brilliant women I know. She possesses an innate ability to maximize her skills of introspection and insight. She ephemerally knows people on a deeper level. Yet, she is often frustrated and lacks confidence in pinpointing a word that was once on the tip of her tongue. Sometimes searching for words results in a blank thought.

I love this woman. I loved her before the stroke and love her now, still. After the stroke. I think this is true of many who have witnessed a loved one struggle with the results of a stroke. Fortunately, Rosetta can speak, walk, swallow, eat, and with little effort, write a text. She can think. She can mostly remember. Yet her cache of words that defined some of what she was, are lost to her.

That's what loss is. Losing someone or something so valuable that is taken for granted until it's gone.

Many people today are dealing with the loss of their voices and/or words. Not from a stroke, but from fear of repercussion from friends, family, and society over political views. I don't know which is worse, more life-changing and more frustrating – the literal or metaphorical loss. Yet thanatologists remind us that a loss is a loss is a loss, and despite the cause, the emotional effects are the same.

For Rosetta, I know her so well that I can often provide her with her own words, the ones she cannot seem to find. I know how she thinks, as well as the language in which she thinks. Both languages.

She is still a logophile, a discerning bibliophile, and always a melophile. She is my soul sister and we share our soul sister's sacred secrets. This one I share with you.

Life of (Sighs)

"A picture is a secret about a secret,
the more it tells you the less you know."
(Diane Arbus)

My clients, if prone to writing, often use journaling as therapeutic homework, either for their own personal growth and/or to share their story with me. Below is a journal entry written by a prolific, insightful client who found a theme when writing her thoughts. I suspect that many of you can identify with the loss of truth and keepers of secrets:

I packed my suitcase as I unpacked my memories with borrowed eyes, in this house I once called home. I try to blink, slowly and purposefully, like a camera shutter, in the hopes of changing the pictures in my mind. It is a futile attempt to rewrite my life. The way I craved it to be. My memories are inherited from conversations between Mother and Zia. I'm unsure if they are truths. But it's all I have.

You see, I grew up in quarantine. This pandemic reminds me of my childhood where I was not allowed to speak or make noise. I never left the house, except on Sundays for dinner at Papa and Nona's. I had learned early and quickly, so when out of the house for a couple of hours, the most I could manage was a whisper. Mother taught me through the use of puzzles, diagramming sentences, and pat-a-cake with prepositions. Always in silence. The only words in my life were closed captions.

You see, Father owned a funeral home and we lived upstairs. Father was a tyrant and Mother feared his anger. Father had posted a list of activities that were allowed and the corresponding times. Below are a few examples:

Vacuum - after 8 pm

Cooking - after 8 pm due to the aroma of the food – it may waft down into the rooms downstairs.

Television - never

Baby crying (me) - NEVER

No shoes.

Mother lived like she was tiptoeing on fragments of unsoftened sea glass on a rocky beach – always in fear. I inherited that fear. Although fraught with guilt, one of the rules that Mother did not obey was the television. I was often placed in front of the television, without sound, for hours; however, the closed captions were available. I learned to read through those closed captions. I also learned that sighs are pervasive in both life and television.

"Rachel, why are you leaving so soon?" (sigh)

"Monica, I'm going to miss you!" (sigh)

When I entered elementary school, the teachers expressed their concern to Mother.

"She doesn't speak. She doesn't participate. We would like to have her tested. We think she is on the spectrum." (sigh)

Today, Mother is gone, following a successful drowning attempt. Father sits in a wheelchair, unable to speak. He watches television in the community room of the nursing home. He reads the closed captions.

I chose an occupation that embraces my silence and my whispers. I became a death doula. It is quiet and usually peaceful at end of life.

Today I've prepared a trip to Brugge, Belgium where my Zia Frankie lies in a hospice bed, in the beguinage. I have not seen nor spoken to Zia in over 20 years. Yet, the nuns found me through social media. I wonder if she knows Mother is dead. Zia Frankie is Mother's identical twin sister, who left her bereft, bipolar, shattered, twin Thomasina to manage on her own with a dominant husband and me, a toddler, while Zia traveled throughout Europe.

During preparation for my exodus, I discovered the only evidence of their communication: postcards from Zia with some of her favorite lyrics. No return address, just postmarks from cities around the world. As I shuffled through the deck of postcards that were in chronological order and wrapped in a rubber band to keep their cumulative messages intact, I noticed a sheaf of papers, rolled up like an old diploma and wrapped in colored ribbon. These papers proved to be Mother's unsent responses to Zia's post cards. Each letter was dated, but they stopped abruptly on the day she was found at the bottom of Narragansett Bay. Contrary to Zia's one-line messages, "If the phone don't ring it's just me," Mother's letters appeared to be rife with emotion and literary quotes. I sighed as I slipped both the letters and postcards into my carry-on bag. A long flight would allow me to give them the attention they deserve.

However, I did notice Mother's closing on a few as the sheaf untangled a bit in the transport.

"Frankie, love you more than air, Thomasina."

"Frankie, give to me your leather, take from me my lace. Thomasina"

Mother preferred her given name, Thomasina, rather than Papa Vincenzo's preference of Tommy.

Zia preferred Frankie to Francesca.

Papa always wanted boys. I was his only grandchild. His last disappointment.

I sit waiting at the window for my Uber driver to arrive and take me to the airport. I notice I am clutching my carry-on bag quite closely, wishing that the unsent correspondence between Mother and Zia might provide me with undisguised truths of secrets unshed. The reading should help me unpack my original memories, although the words I plan to read are still through borrowed eyes. If I choose not to read them, I will remain blind. (Sigh).

Notes:

i. "Life of (sighs)" is copyrighted. (Dias, 2018)
ii. Zia- Italian word for aunt
iii. Death doula – a person who assists in the dying process, much like a midwife with the birthing process.
iv. Beguinage: Nuns and religious laywomen occupy this ancient tranquil complex from the 17th century.

v. "If your phone don't ring it's just me" (Dean Petrella, The Complaints)

vi. "Give to me your leather, take from me, my lace." (Stevie Nicks, "Leather and Lace," 1981)

Part 4

Facing Death

TEN STORIES

The Mortician's Daughter

I t's complicated when you're a girl, even more so when you're the only girl in an Italian family with three brothers. Rosa's father was a second-generation funeral director, and she maintained a tacit understanding that she would be the third generation. As the oldest, she would be the first to join the business.

As a precocious, erudite four-year-old, she learned to read by sounding out words from the obituaries in the local newspaper. Sitting on her father's lap during breakfast, Rosa would beg him to read them aloud as she studied the pictures. Many times, she felt cheated because the information was so brief. Rosa often asked, "Daddy, how could Claire Jones, age ninety-four, only have one paragraph to describe her entire life?" She was often frustrated as well; they never disclosed the cause of death. So, Rosa and her father changed venues and began reading the *New York Times*, where the obituaries were lengthy and full. They did not disclose the cause of death either but offered clues: 'Sam Wiley, age 83, died peacefully at home, surrounded by his loving wife and children. Donations in Sam's name should be made to Hospice.' *Cancer.* 'Abigail Hargraves, age 64, was found dead in her home. Donations may be made to the Diabetes Association.' *Diabetes* – no guessing there. Rosa began to fill in the blanks, recalling Einstein's quote:

"Imagination is more important than knowledge."

By age seven, she advanced from obituaries to corpses. Her mom, the hairdresser for the funeral home, saved babysitting money by taking all four children along when she had to "do a head." Her brothers were not quite as interested, but Rosa was fascinated. She always stood on the kneeler, so she could get the best vantage point. So, this is Jennie Brown, age 54, who died suddenly at home. Heart attack or aneurism.

When her middle school's science curriculum required a science fair project, Rosa embalmed cow hearts. Year after year she submitted an embalmed cow's heart to the fair. Sure, parents rolled their eyes, and everyone complained about the smell, but she stood tall and proud. After all, she was the mortician's daughter.

Rosa's father was magical to her. She remembers a Christmas party where he left her alone and scared, but when she sat on Santa's lap, it was her father's mischievous, blue eyes that winked at her. He had such happy eyes. She also thought her father was famous; after all, every family in town chose her father to bury their loved ones.

As an adult traveling in Rome, she chose to have an engraved gift for her father blessed by the Pope. When she gave the salesgirl at the Vatican gift shop his name, her hands immediately flew over her mouth as tears came to her eyes. "Ah, yes, he buried my sister. Please send him my gratitude. I will never forget him."

One of her most memorable moments occurred at age 12, when she received permission to observe the embalming process. No more cows' hearts for Rosa! She felt she had graduated to the big time. She sat on a folding chair in the doorframe of the morgue (OSHA regulations prevented her from entering). She imagined this was her father's final exam; if she passed this, she would be the first to work side by side with her dad.

That evening at the dinner table, Rosa expected her father to congratulate her and admit it was a test. He didn't say anything. They shared the obituaries in silence until she couldn't wait any longer. "Dad, did you hear what I did today?" He responded, "Yes, good job," in a very staccato voice. "Doesn't it mean I am ready to be a mortician now?" "No." Her excitement was cut short. "No, No!? What do you mean no?" she exclaimed. He put the paper down, took off his reading glasses and calmly stated, "Because you are a girl," as if she should have been aware all along that her gender was a detriment. His logic escaped and devastated her. She would never be allowed to follow in her father's footsteps. Freud's concept of penis envy reared its ugly head. She was so angry! She was misled by a Potemkin dream.

Still, she was driven to make her mark. Still aiming to please her dad, she pursued an alternate dream. Rosa knew her father respected knowledge and education above all. She went on to study English and psychology. When she began to pursue her doctorate, she finally got her father's attention. Finally, he was proud. On the phone with her dad in Florida, they discussed the dissertation and her impending defense. He couldn't wait until he could refer to Rosa as "My daughter, the doctor."

Rosa's dissertation defense was scheduled for a Monday. On the Wednesday prior, she received a phone call from her mom. Rosa's father had choked on a piece of calf's liver while dining with a group of his friends at a favorite Floridian restaurant. He suffered a heart attack due to a loss of oxygen and was on life support. Despite his living will, she begged her mom to keep him on life support until she arrived. February school vacation combined with a driving New England snow made all flights impossible. It was three days before she arrived. Her dad died while on life support, and was waiting for his children, embalmed at a local funeral home.

For the second time in her life, she found herself in a morgue. This time she was old enough to enter, and the man on the slab was her father. He was so cold. They dressed him. Rosa slowly and carefully put his socks and scapula on him. She combed his hair and kissed his cheek. They flew home accompanied by her father in his casket, his funeral scheduled for the following Monday at 10 am. Her doctoral defense was scheduled for 1 pm. She attended the funeral mass, said prayers at the cemetery, and delivered his eulogy. Immediately following the funeral, the limousine drove her to a doctoral defense she doesn't remember. When finished, her committee members asked her to leave the room. When she returned, they each took a turn shaking her hand, saying, "Congratulations, Doctor," and then offered their condolences. Rosa returned to the collation.

Anthony F, age 73, died suddenly in Florida. Donations may be made to the Parkinson's Disease Foundation. A hundred other obituaries, victims of the Station Night Club fire, obscured her father's obituary. As she stared at his mischievous eyes looking back at her from the page, Rosa felt sad, and a selfish disappointment that her father's obituary did not stand alone, allowing her to concentrate on filling in the blanks.

Not the Right Story

A client recently began his first session with the statement, "This is the not the right story." He said this with anger, regret, and a sense of incredulity. Upon further query, he explained that he and his wife had just retired, looking forward to a cross-country trip in their newly purchased camper. They were very excited about the prospect of this long and well-planned journey, which included an itinerary that was months in the making. The camper was packed for a six-month trip, fueled up and ready to go. This was the right story. As they packed some snacks for the trip, his wife began to complain of a canker sore in her mouth which was a bit aggravating. They decided to make a quick stop to the dentist for some topical medication before heading out to the highway. This is where the wrong story begins. My client sat in the driver's seat of the camper as his wife ran in to the dentist's office.

That one visit changed the trajectory of their trip and their lives. The dentist immediately biopsied the sore and diagnosed her with mouth cancer, later to be determined caused by undiagnosed HPV. Their trip across the country was immediately modified to trips to oncology centers around the country: Dana Farber, the Mayo Clinic, the University of Texas MD Anderson Cancer Center, and Sloan Kettering. Each visit was fraught with second, third, fourth opinions and surgeries, chemotherapy, radiation, reoccurrence, and new sores. She died one year later, never having taken their dream trip.

It was one month after her death that my client came to me with his statement, "This is not the right story." He was in shock, angry, feeling guilty and full of blame, trying to make sense of a life that took an unwelcomed, devastating turn.

We all have a story, the right story, that includes plans and dreams, but death requires us to rewrite the chapter and often the entire story. Do not misunderstand me; I do not encourage you to live in an anxiety-ridden state waiting for the next shoe to fall with interrupted thoughts of death. I simply encourage you to be aware that your story, my story, our stories are written in pencil. At any time parts of it can be erased.

I suggest we all live our lives without regrets. Tell people you love them. Don't take anything or anyone for granted. Celebrate the people and the moment, bask in what you have, and be prepared to write a different story.

Be well.

"...Like a Drop of Dew..."

"All things hang like a drop of dew upon a blade of grass."
(W.B. Yeats, "Gratitude to the Unknown Instructors")

The First Mortician's Daughter

It was 1906 when Pauline's father, Angelo, and his older brother, Benedetto, two Italian immigrants from Prata Sanita, Italy, emigrated to the United States and ventured into a funeral business in the small Italian enclave of Silver Lake, Providence. Angelo married Mary, a beautiful Irish girl who became a nurse.

Pauline was born in 1927, the first born and only girl of Angelo and Mary. Her birth was followed soon after by her brother, Bob, and finally her brother, Angelo, Jr. She attended Catholic schools, graduated from Saint Xavier Academy, and went on to marry her husband, Peter. Together they had five children, including a set of twins, and lived a traditional American suburban life.

Pauline worked for an insurance company for a while and was a member of a weekly bowling league. They struggled financially, as all couples did, with Pete as the breadwinner (despite his lofty career as an engineer for a prominent Rhode Island firm) and Pauline a stay-at-home mom.

Pauline was a homemaker, a mom, a loving daughter, and wife. She had her hands full with five children, but she always did her best. And her best was good enough. I have wonderful memories of her at the beach house every summer. She was always one of the most pleasant women I knew, and often treated me like her other daughter.

Fast forward to 2006. Pete died and Pauline sold the home they had lived in for most of their lives. She got an apartment but living alone was not the life for her. She loved people. Her health declined and she entered assisted living in 2016. Still always pleasant and sociable, she made many friends, went to her hair salon weekly, played bingo, and went on field trips. Often, some of her children, 13 grandchildren, and 15 great-grandchildren (pre COVID), brought her joy on their visits. Her daughters often took her for rides, or out to lunch as did her sister-in-law.

Why do I feel the need to tell her story? On the surface her life may seem unremarkable, stereotypical, traditional. I tell you this because she is my aunt. I believe all lives are remarkable simply by their very existence. We all leave a legacy, a piece of ourselves with everyone we meet.

I know all this. I remember. She doesn't. She was transferred to an Alzheimer's unit and sits in quarantine without visitors. Her daughters call and she says she remembers, but the cadence of and hesitancy in her voice tells you she doesn't;

however, there is a piece of Aunt Pauline in her five children, 13 grandchildren, and 15 great-grandchildren. Without her, none of them would exist.

As Yeats proffers, "all things (which I chose to interpret as memories) hang like a drop of dew upon a blade of grass." Memories are a powerful part of who we are, but equally as fragile and potentially temporary, like the dew. What happens when we lose them? Auntie Pauline is still the joyful, happy, and social woman she always was. Yes, it's sad. For us. She doesn't know what she doesn't know.

We hold all her memories for her.

Note: Aunt Pauline passed away on December 18, 2020.

Corona Virus –
Staring into the Sun

A recent research article, written by Sherman Lee et al (2020) in the *Journal of Anxiety Disorders*, coined the phrase "Coronaphobia" and defines it as "a relatively new pandemic-related construct related to functional impairment and psychological distress." It may be comforting to some of you who are struggling with anxiety to know that your feelings are so pervasive, so popular that there is a name for it! A phobia is an extreme fear or aversion to, in this case, coronavirus.

Let's look at where that fear is actually rooted. We know that the virus is contagious, which is scary, and it can be fatal, which is also scary – yet I suspect that Coronaphobia is rooted in our fear of death, the idea of our own mortality, and our struggle to avoid it.

According to world-renowned author and psychiatrist Irvin Yalom, all our anxieties are embedded in death anxiety. Let me repeat: ALL our anxieties are embedded in our death anxiety. In his book *Staring at the Sun: Overcoming the Terror of Death*, Yalom cautions us that "the more unlived your life is, the greater your death anxiety,...[and] sooner or later [we] give up hope for a better past." Yalom also warns us that "self-awareness is what makes us human, but it comes at a price: the wound of mortality. Our existence is forever shadowed by the knowledge that we will grow, blossom...diminish, and die." Finally, Yalom poses a question to all: "Why stare into the sun? Why grapple with the most terrible, the darkest, and most unchangeable aspect of life?" What is your response?

As I type this, I'm reminded of Chloe Benjamin's book entitled *The Immortalists*. In Benjamin's story, four siblings visit a fortune-teller who is said to have otherworldly powers. One in particular is her ability to predict the exact date of their deaths. Each sibling chooses not to share their 'death date' with any of the others, and from there we are offered a view of how each of them is influenced by knowing the day they would die. I wondered how knowledge of our death date might affect our death anxiety. I proffer that, at least in my case, it would decrease anxiety as I feel much anxiety is grounded in the unknowing.

What about you?

I encourage all of you to think about it. Does Coronaphobia increase or decrease when you know your date of death? Does our death anxiety diminish when we have this glimpse into the future? Will you give up hope for a better past? I thought I would reach out to Irv Yalom and ask him. Here is his response:

"Interesting question. I'd vote for it decreasing our anxiety. It would for me." – Irv

And me as well, Irv, and me as well.

ALS

As a child, Gregory watched the young girl next door as she hung out the wash on the clothesline in her backyard. As he grew older, he thought he might be a priest and he created a makeshift church in his basement. The girl next door attended Mass every week. He never became a priest, but he did marry the girl and became a nationally renowned hockey player. He was a star goalie in both Canada and the United States in the days when a helmet was not even an idea in the NHL. He wore a '0' on his uniform because no one could score against him. He was invincible, until ALS became his biggest competitor. ALS, or Lou Gehrig's Disease, is an insidious enemy which affects the ability to walk, speak, swallow, and eventually breathe.

I met Gregory about six months before he died. I sat with him every Friday and watched the NHL cable station. He was still able to talk and walk and he gave me a blow-by-blow description of every play in the game. Eventually we began to watch and play *Family Feud*. He was always such good company.

He called me "Big Gulp" because I always had a 32-ounce drink in my hand when I arrived. His family would go out to do errands while we entertained ourselves and each other.

Gregory had a lift chair that assisted him in getting out of his chair. It worked by a remote control. I sat on a chair directly next to him as he regaled me with stories of the girl next door hanging clothes, and hockey. Always hockey – and the love of his life.

One day I sat in my usual chair and unbeknownst to me I sat on the remote! As I spoke to Gregory, he began to rise along with the chair, until he was over two feet in the air. The two of us shared a very special moment as we laughed hysterically over the situation. It is those moments I remember, those moments I am humbled to be part of.

When Gregory's son came to me sobbing and said, "The nurse said Dad is going to be dead in two weeks," I responded with, "He is going to live for two more weeks! I know you don't feel fortunate right now, but hindsight will shine the light on these two weeks, where you can provide dignity, love, and comfort. You have 336 hours to spend with your dad. And you will treasure those hours forever."

It's odd that I can Google his name and see all the YouTube clips of his famous goalie moves. I never met that young man who had copious amounts of trophies. I met an elderly man with ALS who stole my thoughts with his wit and humor. Each of our moments combined created fond memories that I remember like it was yesterday, even though five years have passed. I can still hear his laughter and his words of wisdom. I have worked with dozens of end-of-life patients since Gregory, but he was one that stole my heart. This article is for

Gregory, his family, and for all who embrace end of life with grace, wisdom and humor.

Call the Death Doula

"I don't know why you say goodbye, I say hello"
(Beatles, "Hello, Goodbye," 1967)

Many of you have watched *Call the Midwife*, either on BBC or more recently on Netflix. Many are familiar with the term "midwife," or "doula" as someone who is trained to assist women in childbirth.

A death midwife or death doula is someone who is trained to assist individuals in their passing from life to death. "Death doulas act as a kind of life coach for those at the end of life. They empower their clients to consider their last years, months, weeks, and even days, carefully and thoughtfully. Our role in reducing fear and regret at the end of life will help them face their last days with increased inner strength, peace, and resolve. (Rachel Gurevich, *A Guide to Becoming a Death Doula* 2019,)

Having recently successfully completed my death doula certification, it seems important to share the details of what we do. According to Rachel Gurevich in her book *A Guide to*

Becoming a Death Doula, "a day-in-the-life of a death doula" may include:

Meeting with a healthy client and their family in the dining room of their home, going over advanced care directives, helping them understand their options for the future, facilitating conversation between the client and his or her family, and helping them get their wishes understood and documented.

Standing vigil by the hospital bedside of a dying client. Creating sacred space for the dying and their loved ones by 'lighting' electric candles, playing soft classical music, reading poetry, or using hospital-approved aromatherapy.

Visiting an elderly client, who has no immediate family living nearby, at their home, making sure their basic needs are being met, creating a plan to meet those needs, offering conversation and companionship, helping with meals or light housework, planning your next visit, and reporting back to the elderly client's family on their father/mother/sister/brother's well-being.

Giving a workshop on what a 'good death' can mean at a local library to a diverse crowd, of all ages and backgrounds. Educating the group on what they can do now—while they are well and active—to ensure they die with dignity and peace.

Conducting a 'living funeral' for a cancer patient at their hospice bedside. Helping plan the event and, on the day of, helping direct the ceremony, and possibly documenting the funeral through pictures or video, or keeping a detailed written record.

Meeting with the friends and family of a recently passed loved one, who left this world suddenly and tragically. Helping them navigate their burial and funeral options, putting them in touch with appropriate resources, educating them on the natural and normal stages of grieving, and creating a plan together on how you can best support them in the coming days and weeks.

Holding the hand of a terminally ill client, and listening to their fears, life stories, and wishes for their end of life. Possibly offering guidance for taking those stories and creating a legacy project, something to help them process and admire the amazing life they have lived and create a physical remembrance of that life.

We also help educate both the patients and their families about the options for disposal. Burial and cremation are the two most popular; however, there are several alternatives. Some little-known options include:

- Resomation: dissolving of the body which turns the body into liquid. Some consider resomation as a greener alternative to cremation.

- Turn the body, or even just a lock of hair, into a diamond (http://www.lifegem.com). We can also become part of a barrier reef (https://www.eternalreefs.com/) or launched into space (https://www.celestis.com/about/).

There are very few limiting factors in the job of a death doula. As noted in a "Day in the Life" above, we can assist in one or all areas described, in addition to serving as a pet doula. I consider myself a sherpa in this role as a death doula. A scout who guides the patient and their families through the oftentimes unfamiliar journey of death and dying. We see our patients as not dying, but rather living for the remaining time, and therein lies the unique perspective we have as we provide dignity, support, and the opportunity for a 'good death.'

The Mortician's Daughter

Reprise

When I die there will be no questions to ask. Why? Because I'm in the business of death and dying and this is what you think about. You plan. I've worked with too many clients who deal with unanswered questions. I've been planning my exit for years, having prearranged my wake, funeral, and burial. Just to make sure it's done right. My way. I've been doing this for over 15 years. My obituary is written in the first person and completed, except for the date of death, and updated along with my resume on a regular basis. It begins with my favorite Mary Oliver quote: *"Tell me what you plan to do with your one wild and precious life?"*

I've chosen my casket (the one with the apostles at the last supper, bronze, with a white interior to match the flowers). Oh yes, the flowers. I will have only white flowers, any kind (but multitudes of them), and one black rose in their midst. The black rose is significant to only a few but suffice it to say it's so memorable to me that I have one as a tattoo.

My hair and make-up will be done by my stylist Aurora, and my lashes by Caitlin. I'm thinking I'll just wear my favorite jeans and a sweater...and my signature boots. (You won't see them because the casket will be closed near my feet, but I'll know I have them on and no one will ever borrow them or give them away). No jewelry. I'm not an earring person and anything valuable will be left to my children – I won't need gold or diamonds in the afterlife. But I may need my boots.

Now for my wake. Given the stereotypical Rhode Island mentality, I plan to have two wakes: one in South County where I reside, and another in Cranston where I grew up. Grievers will have no need to travel. There will be photographs and a streaming video of my life in snippets, lavender diffusers, and subdued lighting.

For my funeral, an honor guard has been chosen (names and contact information on file at the funeral home) to greet my casket as we enter the church. Pallbearers will include my children's friends who spent most of their lives at my house. They are my surrogates.

I struggle with the music, though. I have my vocalist and a few of my favorite tunes ("Come to Jesus" by Chris Rice will make a nice recessional, but I am partial to "When the Saints Come Marching In" (perhaps a bit too jaunty), but I'm sold on the "Battle Hymn of the Republic." I truly love the Beatles song "In My Life," but I've been advised that the Catholic church won't allow it at the church, so I've decided to have it playing at the wake with a few other non-denominational songs. (#The Complaints).

There are so many awesome ways to use cremation remains that I am entertaining a cremation after the funeral, so people can use my ashes in jewelry, mixed in tattoo ink, in the dirt to plant a fledgling tree, or off the Florida Keys, placed by a scuba diver at the Neptune Memorial. I'd like to be part of a reef... although I do love a good graveside service... Perhaps I'll have both.

Now for the tombstone. This is the most difficult of all, as I am a woman who loves words. And there are so many good ones. But after long and arduous thought and research, I've decided on a quote from Nietzsche's *Thus Spoke Zarathustra*:

"Was that life? Well, then once again."
Mari Dias 1952 –

Matthew's Miracle

Both Matthew and his teenage son came down with a cold. The primary care physician gave them an antibiotic and Matthew's son improved within days; however, Matthew did not. Following three weeks of continued flu-like symptoms, Matthew contacted his doctor again. Upon a repeat visit, the physician prescribed a steroid.

Several days later, Matthew was found at home on the floor, unresponsive. 911 was called and upon arrival to the ER, Matthew was intubated. His levels across the board were lethal. His body temperature was 88, his sugars 900, his kidneys were failing, his lungs showed double pneumonia and lesions, (but tuberculosis was ruled out), and his white cell count was in the range with that of a cancer or leukemia patient. Tests indicated it was not an infection. Not coronavirus. Matthew was transferred to the ICU, with doctors indicating it was an hour-to-hour intensive watch to see if he survives.

Matthew was put into a medically induced coma and kept in quarantine for airborne disease. He was released from the coma during the quarantine but with associated delusions, confusion, disorganized speech, and a flight of thoughts. Matthew reports experiencing his "all time low" during this time. He describes this as "a heavy adrenaline rush" or a "re-boot" of his mind. Following weeks of testing and treatment there did not seem to be a diagnosis. The medical community knew what it wasn't, but not what it was. Matthew went through physical rehabilitation and 14 pints of blood following two colonoscopies to determine the location of the bleeding. Following three weeks of hospitalization, Matthew was released from the hospital into his beloved state replete with water and sunshine – two of the most effective climate environments for healing. Matthew survived.

Matthew is a 55-year-old male with four children and three grandchildren (one born while he was hospitalized). Moreover, Matthew is a diabetic. Research on steroids for diabetics indicates problematic issues. Sugars and medications must be closely monitored, as steroids raise sugar levels and require close monitoring to ameliorate risk factors. Perhaps Matthew was in a diabetic coma – and/or experiencing diabetic ketoacidosis. We don't know. But we do know that he is alive and well, albeit frail and thin.

You're probably wondering whether Matthew saw a bright light or visited heaven or spoke to God. We know of the legions of empirical data on the incidence of these reported near-death experiences. Matthew reports that he did not have any visual experiences, but he "felt" God speaking to him, telling him he would survive, and a message to "pay it forward." Matthew also reminds us that hearing is the last to go and warns us about what we say when we are visiting a loved one in a coma. He states that he could hear everything that was said but was unable to respond. ESPN was a welcome sound, but his siblings' tears and sadness brought frustration as he wanted to tell them to stop. He had no way to communicate nor did he know where he was or what had happened. His description reminds me of Jean-Dominique Bauby's description of locked-in syndrome in his book *The Diving Bell and the Butterfly*; however, Bauby could communicate by blinking one eye, the only part of his body that he could move following a stroke.

It behooves us to take care of our health and question our doctors. The physician knew Matthew was a diabetic. Why prescribe steroids without a discussion of the risk factors as well as the medication management for diabetes with steroids? Perhaps the steroids were not a factor – although one must question sugar levels of 900!

There is a saying "Live like you're dying." Matthew learned this the hard way. He agrees that we all think we have more time. Matthew now does have more time. And so, do we. We just don't know how long. It's the dash between our birth date and death date that is important. As Mary Oliver queries, "Tell me, what is it you plan to do with your one wild and precious life?" Make the dash count.

Divine Intervention

Agnes was a spry, energetic 80-something-year-old woman, a tiny woman in both weight and stature, who prided herself on golfing 18 holes three times a week. "Without a cart."

She would overemphasize that phrase. I was the water aerobics instructor, whose class entitled "No Excuses, No Regrets" was a challenge for cross trainers; however, Agnes prided herself in attending my class. Religiously. Consistently. And always following her hair salon appointment. She was the best coiffed participant I had known for years. She was more than a participant. More like a favorite aunt or grandmother.

I taught on the pool deck. Many instructors teach in the pool, but my certification instructor insisted that we teach where we can see participants and correct form and balance. This is impossible if you, as the instructor, are in the pool.

It was a Friday evening class, usually small (about 6-8 participants), and Agnes in the front row, her smiling (and sometimes to other colleagues) smug expression, readying herself for the first sound of a downbeat.

I began the class with a warmup, using the *Grease* soundtrack to begin. I used the big, yellow Styrofoam pool noodle as my microphone, mouthing the words "You're the one that I want."

Then I would offer Agnes the "microphone" and she would respond with, "Oo, oo, oo."

This little "dance" went on for about three minutes, and then I turned to the boom box to increase the volume. When I turned back to face the pool, Agnes was underwater, floating like a dead goldfish, you know, at an angle. I shouted to the other participants who stood frozen and motionless.

"Call nine-one-one."

I immediately jumped in the pool and lifted Agnes by her shoulders to avoid inhalation of water.

It was difficult to get her out of the pool, despite her diminutive size. I remember thinking, there is such a thing as literal dead weight, as I lifted her up the three steps to the pool deck. She was blue-purple, her belly swollen like a pregnant woman ready to go into labor.

I never thought I would remember but I did. All the steps in CPR.

1. Shake the person and call their name.
   "Agnes. Agnes"…no response.

2. Check for a pulse.
   None.

3. Swipe the inside of the mouth for foreign objects to protect choking.

Agnes had false teeth. I removed them and at that point she vomited. The mouth guard was in a closet outside of the pool area. I had no choice.

I began CPR.

The EMTs arrived in less than five minutes. They used the AED-defibrillator. Unsuccessfully. Again. No signs of a pulse. They whisked her away on the gurney, shouting over their collective shoulders, "Call family members. Don't think she is going to make it."

There I stood, soaking wet in my aerobic sweats and sneakers, astounded at what had just happened in the span of less than 30 minutes. I ran to the front desk and asked the manager to access Agnes's emergency contact information and make the call. I was in a hurry to get to the ER.

The manager asked, "Where are you going?"

"To the hospital emergency room."

"Are you crazy? You'd better call a lawyer. You are not employed by this fitness center. You are an outside consultant. Our insurance will not cover you. Get a lawyer."

"I can't. She was like a family member to me. I don't want her to die alone. Her adult children are all out of state. I will sit with her until they arrive."

I raced to the hospital, only to find Agnes on life support and a priest by her side. He was giving her the last rites.

I simply sat and held Agnes's hand until a nurse came in and asked, "The doctors are looking for the aerobics instructor who was teaching at the time."

"Well, that would be me."

The nurse exclaimed, "What are you doing here? You should be in hiding! You are going to get sued!"

I said nothing and continued to hold Agnes's hand.

The nurse had me rise and follow her into a consultation room. A cardiologist and a pulmonologist were waiting for me.

"How long was she underwater...huh, huh? What is your name?

"Mari Dias."

"How long was she underwater?"

"Well, I hate to put a number on it, but it was the amount of time it took for me to turn, raise the volume on the boombox, which was on a table less than three feet away from me, and turn back."

"I'm the one that you want."

Turn, raise volume, turn back for Agnes's oo oo oo...

"Three seconds maybe?"

"Oh, Ms. Dias, it was much longer than three seconds. It was more like 30 minutes. Her lungs were full of pool water. Her heart is fine. She drowned."

I couldn't fathom how this might have happened. She had just returned from dinner at Applebee's. Did she vomit and choke? It is hot and clammy in the pool area. Did she faint and fall underwater?

These thoughts hounded me. "I know it was seconds. I am positive it was just seconds!"

Once again, I was encouraged, this time by the doctors, to call my lawyer.

"You could lose your house, your bank accounts, your husband's business."

I thought. I didn't call anyone.

Agnes's daughter arrived first, about six hours after we had arrived at the ER. She said, "My mother always bragged that she was the oldest person in "Killer Mari's" class, "No Excuses, No Regrets. She died doing what she loved."

The family decided to pull the plug once all the siblings had arrived. That took several days. The cardiologist came in to tell me that, "Upon further testing, it appeared she did not drown; she had an arrythmia. Her heart stopped for a second and she went under."

The family requested my presence when they stopped life support.

I don't know if that was a punishment or a sign of a special place in Agnes's heart.

Once the machines were shut off, we all sat there, still, and quiet. Praying silently. Sometimes it only takes five minutes. Sometimes much longer.

After an hour and a half, we were shocked into reality when we heard Agnes's voice!

"I'm so sorry! Did I cause some mayhem at the fitness center? I didn't mean to…"

Agnes had no brain damage. They inserted a pacemaker about a week later.

One Friday night, about six weeks later, Agnes showed up for Killer Mari's "No Excuses, No Regrets" class.
She sends me a basket of assorted goodies every year on the anniversary and always writes on the card, "Thank you for saving my life. Love, Agnes."

There is no explanation for what happened. She was dead. And then she wasn't. I never called a lawyer. I was never sued. I was thanked. Perhaps if she died it would have been a different story.

But it's not a different story. It is this one.

A Happy Death

"To die, to sleep – To sleep, perchance to dream – ay there's the rub.
For in this sleep of death what dreams may come."
(William Shakespeare)

Griffin was a dear cousin of mine. Like most cousin relationships in the 50's and 60's, we played manhunt and hide and seek in the dark throughout the neighborhood, swam in each other's pools and spent sleepovers on a fairly regular basis. Cousins were like siblings that we didn't live with but maintained close bonds. We were just a year apart and found commonalities in our love of music and dancing. As we reached an acceptable age, we were often seen together on the dance floor of the Rhode Island local clubs.

Griffin received a culinary arts degree and moved to Las Vegas for a head chef position in a large organization. He loved it. His joy of cooking was only surpassed by his joy in watching people enjoy his culinary creations.

One day he went missing. Our uncle and cousins who live on the West Coast searched for him, unalarmed but concerned. It wasn't like Griffin, but they were confident he would return. After a few days of missing work, his coworkers became alarmed. It was not like Griffin to miss an opportunity to cook. They, along with family members, called the local police.

They found Griffin in the desert, curled up in a fetal position, speaking with his deceased grandmother. Griffin returned home with a diagnosis of schizophrenia, which he carried with him until his death. He struggled with the effects of anti-psychotic medication as the voices in his head continued to entertain him. Many schizophrenics experience both visual and auditory hallucinations, oftentimes in the form of persecution or warnings. Fortunately for Griffin, his voices were entertainers, including Las Vegas comedians from one of many of the Las Vegas lounge acts. The Rat Pack appeared regularly as well. Griffin's auditory hallucinations waxed and waned based on the efficacy of his medications; however, throughout the years of trial and error, and new FDA trials, his doctors found a medication with potentially serious side effects but successful in taming the voices.

Once successfully treated, Griffin lived more than three decades of apparent normalcy. Although he remained uncomfortable in groups, he resumed his cooking as we reveled in his expertise. He vacationed in Florida with his family, loved to drive around the state with his brother as they checked out real estate and every Sunday afternoon was spent at a different restaurant with his mom and dad, brother and nieces.

He was a family man. He had a unique close relationship with his mom, my aunt. He enjoyed accompanying her to the supermarket, choosing his favorite ingredients for a special dish.

It was only recently that he began to feel unwell. Not psychologically. Physically. He was hospitalized on and off with a cacophony of diagnoses, each eventually dismissed. Griffin fell into a coma because his ammonia levels were very high. None of the attending doctors knew why. His liver functions indicated possible cirrhosis. I overheard some heartbreaking comments made surreptitiously by health care workers that referred to Griffin as the "sixty-two-year-old alcoholic with cirrhosis." These comments seem to change the trajectory of his care, to his detriment. Less dignity, attention, and respect. The irony was blatant; he was not a drinker. Hospital staff would not acknowledge this fact as it didn't fit their narrative.

Miraculously he came out of the coma; however, his oxygen kept dropping and doctors discussed intubation and respiration measures. While these decisions were weighing on my aunt, my uncle, Griffin's father, was admitted to the same hospital, one floor down from Griffin, for complications from lymphoma. He was temporarily intubated as well. My uncle was discharged with his DNR in hand. Griffin didn't. He was surviving only on life support measures. A decision needed to be made. My aunt decided to stop life support.

We were all at his bedside – about 10 of us, when they took him off the respirator and removed the intubation tube. The nurse said it would only be a short time before he died. Of course, the word 'short' is a relative term. Griffin remained unencumbered by any tubes or machines, seemingly sleeping peacefully. They had not started a morphine drip yet as he didn't seem to be in any pain.

We all continued speaking to him, knowing that hearing is the last to go. An hour passed when Griffin opened his eyes and began speaking to all of us. He asked me what I was doing for the weekend. He told his mom he needed to go shopping for a new suit. He teased his young nieces. Everyone was confused. Was this the last 'rally' medical experts talk about?

Griffin was lucid and alert, despite the decrease in his oxygen without aid. Suddenly he began to look up at the ceiling. The most beatific aura of peace and calm radiated from his face. His skin morphed into that of a baby, untouched, and unwrinkled. His eyes still wide open and still looking at the ceiling, I couldn't help but ask, "Griffin, what do you see?"

Again, his facial countenance changed to an almost ethereal presence. He smiled the most genuine, wide smile when he responded, "Happiness. I see happiness!" shedding tears of joy at the vision he saw. He finally experienced a state of being that had previously been elusive.

He closed his eyes and the nurse asked if she could give him some morphine to expedite his death. My aunt agreed, and then found herself distressed just sitting there, waiting for her son to die. She decided to leave, and along with her everyone did the same. I felt compelled to stay. I didn't want him to die alone, although I know that some wait for everyone to leave before they go. We choose the moment.

Ten minutes after everyone left, while they were all still in the parking lot preparing to leave the hospital grounds, Griffin took his last breath. I felt compelled to wash his feet with a warm cloth, moisten his already drying lips. I spent a few minutes alone with him and called the funeral home to send someone to transport Griffin. I then made a special request. Most times, the deceased body is sent down to the hospital morgue to wait, along with dozens of others, for transport. This wait can take hours. I wanted my cousin to be picked up in his hospital room, in his bed. A more dignified transport. My request was honored. I waited while the nurses washed his body and put his toe tag on his newly cleansed feet.

They covered him with a crisp, white sheet. When they covered his face, I protested. The nurses acquiesced. I sat with Griffin for over an hour. He was gently and lovingly transported to the funeral home, never having spent one minute in one of the drawers in the morgue as a simple number.

Hindsight is 20/20. Even in medical assessment and diagnosis. Griffin's death certificate indicated the cause of death was cirrhosis of the liver caused by decades of daily ingestion of the new age antipsychotic that balanced him and gave him a modicum of a normal life. This was not included in the long list of side effects. Yet, if it had been included, would it have made a difference?

Rest in peace, Griffin. I know you experienced a happy death.

NOTE: Griffin's father died two months following Griffin. Uncle was sitting in his favorite recliner watching the news when he said, "I have to go and take care of my son."

Rest in peace, Uncle.

Part 5

Perspective

FIFTEEN STORIES

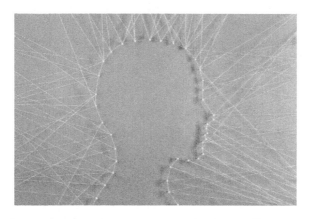

What Would You Do?

I'm the type of person who is likely to ask for forgiveness rather than permission. Am I always forgiven? No. Does that discourage me? No.

There are so many examples of this that I could write the great American novel, but the story below may provide sufficient evidence.

I was teaching a psychology course at a small New England college. It was Friday afternoon, last class of the day. As I dismiss my students, Neil saunters up to my podium and offers up his plans for the weekend.

"Hey Dr. D! Hope you have a great weekend!"

"You as well, Neil. Any plans?"

"Well, now that you mention it, Dr. D, yes. I have the keys to my father's gun cabinet and my parents are away for the weekend."

I took a deep breath, quieting my response, but it had no effect on the quick jerk of a thousand thoughts in my mind. I thought, *This is a cry for help. What do I do?*

Fortunately, my thoughts answered me immediately.

Under no circumstances can you allow Neil to go home. Get him to the school psychologist.

"Okay, Neil, that's quite a weighty statement. Sounds like you have a plan to suicide. I cannot let you go home. Let's take a walk over to Dr. Steve's office."

"No, Dr. D. I'll speak with you, but I'm not going to see Dr. Steve."

We left the building together and walked and walked in circles around the campus, with me hoping against hope that when we neared Dr. Steve's office Neil might change his mind. He didn't.

Before long, darkness was imminent, and Neil was in a heightened stage of emotional distress. He had shared his life of abuse and neglect, as well as the bullying throughout high school. He didn't seem to know how to fit in and hated being different. He just wanted it all to end.

Soon the automatic outdoor campus lights came on and it began to rain. I could not let him go home. He wouldn't go to Dr. Steve, all the buildings were locked for the weekend, and faculty are not allowed to have students in their cars (for any reason). A conundrum for sure.

Society says if we follow the rules there will be no undue consequences. I was aware of all the potential consequences, willing to accept them (even if I lost my job) because I was saving someone's life. Neil joined me in my car in order to continue talking and remain dry.

He was knee deep in depression and crying uncontrollably. We sat. We talked. We sat. We talked. The rain stopped. He agreed to see Dr. Steve. Thankfully, Dr. Steve's office light was still on, an offer of hope for both of us. I introduced Neil and Dr. Steve and left, still holding onto the weight of Neil's distress and also a bit relieved that Neil was finally in the right place.

Fast forward to Monday. I arrived for my morning class early, only to find a message from the dean. She wanted to see me as soon as possible.

Perhaps she wants to thank me, I thought, as I headed over to her office. I was met with an academic firing squad of innuendos, outright accusations, and admonishments for my actions.

"Dr. D., what gives you the right to take a student's mental health issues and address them? Particularly on school property?"

She's not going to thank me, that's for sure, I thought when I heard her opening statement.

"I saved his life. I let him speak. Calm him down. He felt listened to, less hopeless. He was going to use one of his father's guns to kill himself."

"Well, that is not your role, nor your responsibility, Dr. D. You are a professor. Professors teach. Professors do not counsel. It is not in your contract. In fact, the faculty manual explicitly states, 'No faculty, under any condition, may allow a student in their personal vehicle.'"

"Yes, I'm aware of that rule, but I did what I felt was right. Ethically. Morally. I chose integrity and aspirational ethics over the rules. I have a private practice as well and have malpractice insurance which I concluded was sufficient enough to speak to Neil."

"We have counselors here, and it is not in your job description! We could get sued if he went home and shot himself after speaking to you on college property! If you cannot follow the rules, we have no choice but to terminate you. And next time, if there is a next time, as many would not hire you with this behavior on your record, if this occurs, please tell the student to meet you at a coffee shop down the street so that your university is not culpable."

That was the end of my seven years teaching psychology at a small New England college.

Did I second guess myself? Not for a minute.

Was the university sued? No, because Neil did not shoot himself.

Would I do it the same way again, knowing the outcomes? Absolutely.

Some might say that it is my privilege that allows me to be civilly disobedient. Civil disobedience is not always about pillaging, rioting, and looting. Sometimes it is about going against an unfair rule or law, for the good. Could I financially afford to lose my job? No. But I couldn't not do what I did and live with myself.

I didn't ask for permission, and in the end, I asked for understanding. I didn't need or want their forgiveness. My conscience was/is clear.

When I applied for a teaching position at another university, they asked me why I left my former teaching position after seven years. I told them the truth. I told them the story.

"If the same situation occurred at our university, would you make the same choices?"

"Yes, and if this university would respond in the same way, it's not the place for me."

They wouldn't. I was hired, not in spite of, but because of my strong ethical stance.

What would you have done?

Memento Mori

"The choice was made
Plans were laid
To exit life
To end this strife
Ingest the pills
Depression kills
You fade away
So still you lay
Fading into darkness
Into an endless sleep
But wake to find yourself alive
You have failed at suicide."
(Tearstained, "Failed Suicide Attempt," 2003)

It was a Tuesday morning, and I was on my way to speak at the National Association of Death Education and Counseling annual conference. I was excited with the anticipation of speaking to this lofty group. I had been waiting years for one of my proposals to be accepted for presentation, and this was my big chance. Unfortunately, my flight from Providence was delayed 45 minutes. Then an hour. Then two hours. Then, waiting for a substitute plane. Finally, we were on route. I anticipated missing my connection in Atlanta. Once we landed, I ran through three concourses to my connecting gate. Fortunately, my connection was late as well.

I sat down at the cell phone station to charge my phone, confused as to why I was almost out of battery so early in the day. As I plugged in my phone, I noticed a text message that was posted one minute earlier.

It was a former client who simply wrote, '64 Xanax.'

What?! I thought. *What about 64 Xanax?*

I texted her back, still tethered to my charging table. Simultaneously the announcement for boarding to my final destination came on through the microphone.

"Those with the letter 'A' may board."

That was my letter, but I didn't move. I waited for her reply, which never came.

I was flustered and overwhelmed at what I perceived as two conflicting demands – get on the plane or call 911. I soon realized I could achieve both; however, I did not have an address for the client, although I did have an emergency contact number. I called her daughter and then texted her. I was met with a voice message and silence. By this time, I was in my seat, my seatbelt fastened, ready for takeoff. The flight attendant was annoyed with me and repeatedly told me to get off my phone. I told her it was an emergency. She didn't care.

I deplaned. I thought of what I emphasized to my students. The Counselor Code of Ethics stresses 'Do no harm' and includes definitions of both mandatory and aspirational ethics. I strive for aspirational ethics. This woman's life was my priority. Once again, I found myself running through the airport terminal, this time in search of a return flight to Providence. Success. I ran to a gate that indicated a future flight to Providence, all the while calling and texting her daughter.

I left a message. "Your mom has taken an overdose of Xanax. I've called 911 but I don't know her address. The police and EMTs are trying to locate her."

Just as the attendant notified me that the next flight to Providence was in 30 minutes, my phone was ringing. Serendipity.

It was my client's daughter. She received my messages and texts, but thought I might be exaggerating, so she went home to check on her mom. She found her slumped halfway off her bed, wedged between the bed and the night table. She was unresponsive. She called 911 with the correct address. The EMTs arrived, gave her mom a shot of Narcan and acknowledged the empty bottle of pills and an almost empty bottle of tequila.

The woman was rushed to an ICU bed at a local hospital, where she was first given charcoal and then intubated. There she remained for several days. Once she was able to breathe on her own, she was transferred to a local residential treatment facility for help with the emotions that led up to the suicide attempt.

The flight back to Providence seemed endless. Upon arrival, I found myself running, once again, this time to a waiting Uber to take me to the hospital. The airline was worried about my luggage. Apparently, it had taken the route of my planned itinerary and was waiting impatiently at my final destination. Not my priority.

My former client survived. We learned later than she had been stockpiling the Xanax for a day like that Tuesday. She knew it was only a matter of time. The tequila came first and offered a mode of disconnection, some kink in her cognitive processes. Taking the entire bottle of pills seemed like the rational action.

I remain incredulous over the wonder of the universe and its synchronicity. I found myself caught up in the miracle questions. *What if my first flight was not delayed?* But it was. *What if my connecting flight was not delayed?* But it was.

Where would I have been at 12:20 pm that day if it had gone as planned? I would have been in flight to my final destination, never having seen the text until I landed. That would have been too late.

As often as these things happen, I still am amazed at the outcome. I had a five-minute window to charge my phone and noticed the text. It was meant to be.

She claims I saved her life. Perhaps I assisted in saving her life – yet she texted me. Why? It doesn't matter. She was either reaching out, or warning, or preparing me. In any event, she is here. Many are not.

My best advice is to reach out to someone. We know that most people regret their decision within minutes of taking action. There is no room for guilt and shame, even after the deed is done. Text someone, let them know. This world is empty without you, you know.

Zulu Time

I n today's world where extreme political correctness, hate, vitriol, and lack of empathy are rife, I decided to go to a happy
place. If we remind ourselves, we all have the capacity to do
so. In my search for a happy place I was pleased and surprised
that I had so many to choose from! In that sense I am privileged,
although anyone who knows me is aware that I take every opportunity to "suck the marrow out of life" (John Keating in *Dead
Poets Society*), seizing every opportunity to learn and engage. Or
maybe it doesn't take much for me to be happy. I reviewed the
laundry list in my mind of all my joyful moments, and with the
memories came the ability to experience, with the same degree
of intensity, the emotions that I felt in the initial moment.

The review of my list took quite a while, as I had to stop
after each one and embrace the feelings. It's like cleaning out an
old drawer only to find pictures that had been stowed away for
a long time. What a treasure! It takes hours to re-remember and
taste the pure happiness that each memory represents.

Today I stopped on a picture in my mind's eye of my experiences in South Africa. It changed me. It humbled me. It opened my eyes even wider than before. Allow me to explain.

I received a Fulbright Specialist Scholarship to the University of Zululand in KwaZulu Natal. Much to my chagrin, I was to arrive two weeks after the academic year ended. This meant that students could not return home after a year of living on campus, until my workshops had ended. My western mind visualized a classroom of students, majoring in social work, to be irate, disengaged, and angry. They would all be sitting at their desks, on their phones, oblivious to my words. I assumed they would all be commiserating among themselves about their shortened summer break.

Not so. It still stops me short when I think about how naïve and encapsulated in my western view I was.

It was a long trip, which gave me too much time to think and perseverate over my expectations.

I flew from Boston to Johannesburg, then a flight to Durban where university representatives greeted me. A two-and-a-half-hour car ride concluded at the apartment that was assigned to me on campus. I looked around. There was nothing. We were in the bush, with only a towering, concrete building to insult the landscape of moba trees (sugar cane).

I had a sleepless night, awakened intermittently by the strange animal and bird sounds to which I was unaccustomed. In the morning, I walked over to the academic building and found the room in which I was to present was locked. I panicked. I needed to set up! I asked for Safety and Security to unlock my room, at which time I was told by a groundskeeper that they had not arrived yet. My anxiety was increasing exponentially. I went over to the dean's office. She hadn't arrived yet, either.

Well, they don't seem to think my visit is very important. I thought.

What did I get myself into?

At last, the dean arrived (30 minutes later) and unlocked the door. Soon students began pouring in – yet they were laughing and smiling and excited, completely contrary to my expectations.

The dean rose, introduced me, and stated, "Before we begin, let us have some tea." Out comes a silver tea service for 25 people, with triangles of ham and cheese sandwiches. I just kept looking at my watch. Ruminating. Panicking.

Following our teatime, the dean introduced a student who read a message to me on behalf of the entire class:

"Dear Dr. Dias, We are so humbled, honored, and graced by your presence. The fact that a white woman from America would travel halfway around the world to educate poor, black women in a developing third world country is very special to us."

"Ubuntu." (essential human virtues of compassion and humanity)

My eyes welled with tears of humility and gratitude. There were no cell phones. There wasn't any dissension or frustration. They were honored!

My workshop began two hours later than its original start time. Students all asked to take pictures with me, pleaded for my autograph, and put me on the proverbial pedestal higher than anyone deserves to be held.

I visited 'places of safety,' which are orphanages for children from birth to 18 who are victims of the virgin cleansing cure. (Legend has it that having sex with a virgin will cure one of AIDS). I toured the prison, interviewing those incarcerated for raping children, and a local Christian Mass, which they conducted in the Zulu language, but when I arrived, they translated everything to English as well.

I joined families in their homes for a *brea* (cookout) and every morning I was greeted by a collective shout of *"Saubona!"* (good morning) from the students.

It was difficult to leave. During my going away party, the dean approached me and shared her observations.

"You always seem to be in a hurry. No need here. We are on Zulu time. Did you eat? Is the sun shining? Are you well rested?"

"Yes."

"Then that's all that matters. Everything else will take care of itself."

Today, this is my happy place of memories seared into the fabric of who I am.

Let's give pause to this world view. Let's all embrace the philosophy of *ubuntu* and live on Zulu time. Even for an American minute.

Tree of Life, Gustav Klimt

Grieving Youth

"For age is opportunity no less
Than youth itself, though in another dress,
And as the evening twilight fades away
The sky is filled with stars, invisible by day."
(Henry Wadsworth Longfellow,
"For Age is Opportunity No Less")

My refrigerator was once covered with report cards, class pictures, and kid's schedules. Today it is dressed in prayer cards, doctor's appointments, and laminated obituaries. My morning coffee is accompanied by the yearning for days gone by as I am welcomed by these faces, long and most recently gone.

Each and every loss reminds me of the past, along with the memories that I shared with them. I still hold the memories in my pocket, accessible when needed. Yet the other half of the memories have been cremated or buried along with those who shared them. I have fewer years in front of me than behind me.

I yearn for my youth. It's not lost, just passed. I grieve "my lost loves, lost health, lost capacities" (Tara Brach). I miss the long nights and short days, of dancing until midnight and the ability to jump up the next morning without exhaustion. I miss the physical energy I had, the paucity of time it took to do my hair and makeup. Today, the efforts to hide the wrinkled face and crepey skin, and general upkeep is time consuming; however, what I miss most are the people of my youth. They are all entangled with my memories of youth, and without them the memories fade just a bit, enough to have me attempting to recall each and every one, in an effort to make the memories brighter, as rich as they once were.

But there are few with which I can relive these memories. With each passing year, their numbers decrease, as I struggle with the fading recall of my younger years. Perhaps I employ the halo effect, as I recapture and indulge in this journey, remembering only the good times.

And yet, I feel young. When I look in the mirror I try to disregard what I see and if I squint a bit I can morph the reflection into the younger me. But only for a few minutes, like a scrying mirror for the past. Then reality sets in. I'm not sure if it's vanity or the evidence of a long life that I want to erase.

Unlike Dorian Gray, I am unwilling to sell my soul to remain forever young. That is too big of a price. Yet it doesn't soften or negate the yearning for my youth, for days gone by.

According to many experts, particularly Alan Wolfelt, a world-renowned author of books on grief, "Ageism is alive and well in North America. It is an attempt to distance oneself from the realities of aging, illness, death, and grief." We can avail ourselves of all the possibilities of extending a youthful appearance.

There is Botox, and injections, wrinkle fillers, hair coloring, face lifting, and teeth whitening.

We can run but we cannot hide. Growing old is inevitable. According to many, it may be inevitable but provide us with insight, discernment, and empathy. They view aging as an offer of a gift.

I haven't gotten to that point yet. I need to yearn, to embrace this unwanted gift, to mourn my youth and accept the aging me. It is sometimes very painful, anxiety-provoking and depressing. Those "grave-bound traits and falling features" ("Sunday Girl," Dean Petrella) are a difficult reality to accept, as they signify the time that has passed, seemingly much more quickly than it did when we were young. Long, languid days have segued into weeks that pass in the blink of an eye.

Lost youth seems like lost time. And lost time is scary. So, I will attempt to focus on the here and now. Focus on what I have rather than what I've lost. After all, I'm not dead yet.

"And when I die
And when I'm dead, dead and gone,
There'll be [two children and thousands of students and clients}
in
A world to carry on, to carry on."
(Laura Nyro, "And When I Die," 1972)

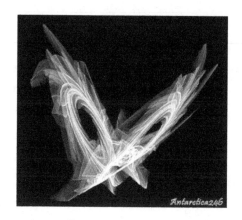

Antarctica246

The Butterfly Effect

"A small change can make much bigger changes happen;
one small incident can have a big impact on the future."

The senseless brutality and ultimate murder of George Floyd perpetrated by Derek Chauvin is no small change, not one small incident in the eyes of many. Yet, in the scheme of things being an entire country or an entire world, one senseless death is considered a small incident. Everything is relative. I firmly believe that when Derek Chauvin held George Floyd down on the ground with his knee on his neck, he never suspected that this one action, that one incident, would prove to be the impetus of protests and riots, additional murders, looting, and millions of dollars spent on maintaining state curfews with police department personnel and the national guard. All because of something he did. Something he is responsible for.

I wonder what he's thinking as he sits in his cell. When he sees the news. He must be astounded to realize that his one action caused this worldwide reaction. How can one man cause this chaos?

It's the butterfly effect.

I'm sure that young teenager who showed up at a protest somewhere in a city, in a state, who saw his friends throwing rocks, would not consider his minor involvement as a cause of someone's financial and social demise. He only threw one rock.

But that rock was the final one that broke the window which provided access into the building. The building is a family-owned restaurant, closed for months due to COVID-19. The family was struggling financially with the close of their 40-year-old business. They tried to make ends meet until 'Phase 2' opened up restaurants. They worked hard to meet all the guidelines, separating tables, and measuring the distance between the chairs. They instituted all the protocols. Their first night open was a resounding success with 50% of the patrons inside the restaurant and 50% dining outside. They did everything right.

The next evening there was a protest, which morphed into a riot, and that young teenager threw the last rock that broke the window and allowed dozens of others to get into the property. Tables and chairs were thrown against the wall, broken, the bar with its mirrored background and shelves, demolished. The family can't go on any longer. They have nothing left to repair the building.

The parents divorce after daily arguments, the daughter goes out on the streets, confused and alone and takes a pill offered to her. It will make her feel less lonely. Less scared. Her world, her family is not what it was and never will be. It was fentanyl and without Narcan available, she dies. Her older brother, who is taking the family breakup worse than his sister, is fraught with guilt and remorse. He feels like he's the man of the family now and he failed. He hangs himself a week after his sister's death.

Am I being overly dramatic? No. True story.

It's the butterfly effect.

Am I saying that one small change or one small incident on my part, on your part, could have a big impact, make much bigger changes happen? Indeed I am.

I'm sure that there are not too many of us out there who want this kind of responsibility. We don't want the potential power to create a ripple effect. We don't want to live in paranoia, perseverating over every action and the potential ramifications. I understand.

I invite you to take a moment when you are about to do or say something and think about the unintended consequences. Ask yourself: Do I want this word or action to create a bigger change, have a bigger impact on many? If your response is no, then rethink it. If your answer is yes, be my guest. You will be one of the changes we see in this world.

I embrace this type of responsibility. It makes me feel needed, important. That what I do can affect many, for the good or the bad. I'll go with the good.

It's the butterfly effect.

DNA Tests –
A Loss or Gain of Cultural Identity?

How many of you have taken the Ancestry or 23andme DNA test? Initially most folks considered this technology with a suspicious eye: today it seems to be de rigueur. However, many people are not expecting or equipped to hear the results.

Stories abound of legacies erased in the time it takes to read the report. This was the case for my client, Nora. Nora is a fifty-something-year-old woman, an only child of Italian immigrants. She grew up in an Italian neighborhood in Chicago, where her parents instilled in her the cultural traditions and values of their culture. She learned to make her pasta by hand, and a traditional Italian "gravy" (not sauce!) and celebrated *La Vigilia di Natale* (Feast of the Seven Fishes on Christmas Eve).

Last Vigilia, Nora received an Ancestry DNA kit. On a lark, she sent her DNA back in the test tube provided and forgot about it. Six weeks later she was surprised and delighted to receive her DNA report. Once she read the report, her surprise and delight morphed into confusion.

Well, this has to be wrong, she thought. The results revealed that Nora was 50% Jewish. How was this possible? Nora had recently applied for Italian dual citizenship and she had culled a great deal of historical information on both her parents. She chalked it up to an error – until she spoke to some friends who encouraged her to pursue the mystery. Nora's parents could not shed any light, as they had passed, but she did have a cousin on her father's side. She bought him an Ancestry kit, only to find his results indicated 100% Italian. Hmm…did her mother have an affair?

Nora remembered that her mother often spoke about her boss at a shoe factory where she worked as a newly married woman, a gentle man who allowed her to work her own hours. Nora also had a vague memory of her maternal aunt suggesting that her mom had a crush on this man. He was much older than Nora's mom. Nora took on the role of sleuth.

She researched the shoe factory, found out the gentleman's name and contacted his family. Sure enough, the father who had raised her was not her biological father. Her biological father was a wealthy Jewish man who owned a factory in Chicago and had died months after her birth. She was shocked. Did her father know? Did her biological father know? How did her mother hold onto this secret for over 50 years? Or did she?

Nora searched for clues in her mother's belongings but found nothing – except a cancer sore on her tongue. She found out her father was not her biological father, and that she was 50% Jewish, a few weeks before she discovered she had tongue cancer. She joked, "My mother is so angry with me for disclosing her secret to everyone that she sent the tongue cancer as a curse to stop me from talking!" (Italians can understand the humor of that statement – "I'll cut your tongue out if you say that one more time!" or "I'll wash your mouth out with soap" are both common reprimands for swearing or talking back to an Italian mother!)

Since Nora shared this story, I've heard dozens of similar ones. Hundreds of people are discovering that the people they considered parents, siblings, or children, are not.

And there's the rub. What does one do when they experience the initial shock? Fortunately for Nora, she eventually embraced her Jewish identity while maintaining her Italian heritage. Others may not be so resilient, and struggle with their cultural identity.

We usually do not associate non-finite loss with Ancestry or 23andMe DNA tests. Given the popularity of these tests, perhaps we should. It is fascinating to search our family tree, to follow our lineage back to its beginnings and learn about generations of people who share our DNA. Perhaps the kit should come with a black box warning label: *Caution: These results are accurate. Be prepared for the truth.*

Postscript: Following several surgeries and cancer treatments, Nora is cancer-free. The majority of her tongue is intact, and she still tells her story to both her Jewish and Italian friends and family.

What's In a Name?

Depression can be as fatal as cancer.

One of my favorite childhood bedtime stories was an old Italian legend that I called 'the miracle story.'

Once upon a time, in the Civita hills in Itri, Italy, a deaf-mute cowherd lost one of his cows. He panicked and began to search high and low throughout the hills, only to stumble upon a rather strange sight. He found his cow kneeling at the foot of a great oak tree. The cowherd knelt beside the cow and from that vantage point he noticed a painting nestled in the branches. Upon further inspection he was surprised and pleased to discover that he recognized the woman in the painting. It was the Blessed Mother and she seemed to be smiling at him. And with that smile he immediately regained his hearing and speech. He was so excited that he ran all the way down the Civita hills to tell all the villagers what had occurred. The date of this miracle was July 21, 796.

The villagers were astounded when they heard the young boy speak and followed him back up the hills to see the painting for themselves. Sure enough, the painting was exactly where the boy had found it. The villagers gently and reverently removed the painting from the oak tree and carried it in procession to the main church in their village of Itri. The next morning, the villagers were astonished to find that the picture was missing from the church. No one admitted to having removed it, so they traveled back up the Civita hills, and there the painting was in its original location, between the branches of the oak tree. The villagers then understood that Our Lady, the Virgin Mother, wished to be honored in the small place where she had originally appeared. A chapel was then built on the site of the tree and called the Sanctuary of Civita.

In 1527, the plague descended on Itri and killed most of the population. In despair, the villagers brought their prayers to the Madonna Della Civita. A large crowd gathered at her sanctuary on July 21 and carried the sacred painting in a procession throughout the villages of the surrounding area, all the while begging the Madonna to free the people from the Black Death. Suddenly a dark cloud was seen emerging from the earth and dissipating into the sky. The plague ended. Ever since then, July 21 is the solemn feast day of the Madonna Della Civita. About half a million pilgrims come each year to this holy place.

In Itri itself, there are three days of local festivities and religious processions. The silver statue of the Madonna and Child, both wearing golden crowns adorned with precious stones, are carried through the streets of town on a golden throne. The procession concludes at the top of Mount Civita. Villagers celebrate the feast with fresh figs, black licorice root, and fireworks. All businesses and schools close and the villagers run through the streets of Itri to catch a greased pig.

Shortly after World War II, many people left Itri and the hills of Civita, emigrating to America, many to Cranston, Rhode Island. They brought with them their culture and tradition and continued to celebrate the Madonna Della Civita on July 21 of each year. Businesses and schools closed, they chased a grease pig throughout the city of Cranston and created a 600-lb. reproduction of the statue of Maria Santissima Della Civita for the annual procession at St. Mary's Church. Since 796, the Madonna continues to provide miracles, beginning with the miracle of the deaf and mute cowherder. It is said that you cannot leave the feast until you have touched the statue of the Blessed Mother, for she will grant your miracles.

The end of the story was my favorite part. "Mary, you were born over a thousand years later, the same date that the deaf-mute cowherd found the painting of the Blessed Mary. While the fireworks from the feast of Madonna Della Civita graced the sky in Cranston, Rhode Island, Mommy gave birth to you. Your birth on the day of the feast is a sign, a minor miracle as we gave you the beloved name of Mary. You are meant for great things." Eight weeks later I was baptized Mary, with all the pomp and circumstance accorded to a chosen one.

I attended the feast of the Madonna every year, touched the statue and asked for miracles. I also attended Catholic elementary school, where I was chosen to be the "Queen of the May" during the feast of the Blessed Mother. I expected to be treated as the chosen one at school as well, except for a physical anomaly that symbolized demonic possession in the Catholic church. I was left-handed. It became the nun's duty to exorcise the demons in me by making me right-handed. I experienced daily beatings with rulers, yardsticks, anything that would result in bloody knuckles, rendering me unable to write with the "devil's hand." To ensure this metamorphosis, my left hand was tied behind my back as well. The beatings resulted in a child's simple conundrum: How can I be the chosen one, born on the feast of the Madonna, given her name, yet beaten daily for my left-handedness?

Eventually I morphed into a rebellious child, which resulted in 'inappropriate and disrespectful behavior.' I was in the third grade when my name began to appear on the blackboard, included in the daily list of students who had detention. I remember looking at the list one day and noticing that almost every name listed was Mary or John. Suddenly I felt common, ordinary, unexceptional. I spent an afternoon trying on different spelling variations of my name. I finally settled on Mari. I was pleased with my altered spelling identity and when I saw Mari on the list for detention, I was proud. My new moniker became a symbol of defiance, an alias that to my family meant I did not value my legacy to the Madonna. They cajoled, yelled, prayed, all in vain. At times I felt like I was faced by an ecumenical council, but I refused to relinquish my restored uniqueness. They, in turn, refused to acknowledge the new spelling and kept it a secret from the family. My grandmother died in her eighties, never knowing about the "i." Even an imprimatur from the pope wouldn't have changed their views. I was no longer chosen; I was a sinner.

However, in the hindsight available only in adulthood, is it not the bloody knuckles or my identity crisis that fills me with dread, panic, and fear, but the sight of a black limousine. Sociologists might refer to it as a symbol, psychoanalysts as a trigger, behaviorists a stimulus. To me, that black limousine meant only one thing. I would not be taking the bus home, chatting with my friends as we walked to our respective homes. I would not walk into the house welcomed by the smell of garlic browning in oil, or my mom stirring the pasta, the steam circling her as she stood by the stove. No, the limousine was there because my mother was in the hospital.

Whenever my mother was rushed to the hospital, my father would pick us up in the funeral home car and take us to Nana's house. When I saw the black limousine I was scared, emotionally dislodged, hating the unpredictability of the predictable. However, my classmates were very impressed with this frequent occurrence, and although they teased us about being rich, the envy in their taunts was palpable. I just wanted to shout at them, beg them to stop, because this sleek, black, shiny limousine was not a sign of social status. It was my nemesis.

I loved the bus. The bus meant everything was common, ordinary, and unexceptional. One day I was taking the bus home, reveling in the normalcy. When I arrived home, an ambulance was parked in the driveway. It seemed the time elements had overlapped, and the limousine driver didn't have time for proper notification. As I walked up the driveway, the attendants were carrying Mom out on a stretcher. I attempted to say hello, but she was unresponsive. I stood catatonic as one of the wheels of the stretcher rolled over my foot. I thought, *so this is the picture I missed while sitting in class, my eyes darting from the clock on the wall to the window, praying the bell would ring at the sight of a fat, yellow, happy bus and not the sleek, shiny black limousine. Perhaps I should have touched the statue more often, prayed for different miracles.* Later my dad told me that this time was serious, and I would have to take care of my brothers.

This would be a long hospital stay and we would not be going to Nana's house. He said Mom was in the hospital and she was receiving a treatment to make her forget about all the things that made her sad and help her to stop crying all the time.

In my childhood mind's eye, I pictured one of the erasers that the boys had to clap at the end of the school day. Maybe this "treatment" was an eraser that would simply make all the sad things disappear, like the names on the board for detention. And when she came home, she would be happy. In adulthood, I now know the treatment was electric shock therapy, a more advanced method of erasure.

When I was 12, I was old enough to visit my mother. As I entered her room, she looked quizzically at me and said, "What a pretty little girl! What is your name?"

I answered, "Mari, spelled with an "i.""

Auld Lang Syne

Hindsight is 20/20. And so is this new year. It is not merely a new year but a new decade, and if social media is any indication, people have varying views on this calendar transition. The posts often begin with hindsight, looking back at the graduations, weddings, births, travels, and deaths, and morph into a hopefulness for the future.

"Boy, oh boy, 2020 kicked me and knocked me down. Hope 2021 treats me better!" (anonymous Facebook user)

"It has been an awesome year! Actually, an awesome decade! Hope 2021 is equally as awesome!" (anonymous Facebook user)

The memes and giphys reflect empowering, proactive suggestions: "This is a new chapter. Write a good one." When we open a Facebook post or an Instagram picture, we are likely to see fireworks, people celebrating with paper hats and over-sized 2021 eyeglasses, kissing the moment the ball drops. Videos show crowds of people singing "Auld Lang Syne," a song whose history indicates that it's usually sung on New Year's and at funerals. (Scotland.org)

For many, it's a birth of sorts. A new beginning. But not for all. Not for the grievers. It may signify the end of something, even if has been 10 years. Be sensitive. Be kind.

According to the Association of Death Education and Counseling, "People don't often think of New Year's as a grief holiday; however, for many, it is the first of a new year in which their loved one does not physically exist…the first true year they [do] not share in together. It is a genuine challenge. Resolve to be gentle with one another."

VITAS Healthcare concurs. "When we are grieving, it is hard enough to live each day as it comes. It can be a daunting task to face a whole new year stretching out in front of us." VITAS goes on to express the potential feelings of the grieving, as they may feel afraid, lost, and no longer busy with caretaking. They proffer the idea that a new year may mean different things to different grievers. Some may welcome, some may dread, and some may ignore the new year, depending on where they are in the grief process. "The question is not whether, but how, we'll work with it."

VITAS Healthcare concludes their article with tips to face the new year.

1. Get needed rest. Grieving is exhausting.

2. Give yourself a mental rest. Soothe yourself with music, prayer, tears, and laughter.

3. Pay attention to hopes and desires.

4. Attend a support group and share memories.

5. Seek spiritual support.

6. Find courage to live into the future by living in the present, one day at a time. (https://www.vitas.com/family-and-caregiver-support/grief-and-bereavement/holidays-and-grief/facing-the-new-year-when-you-are-bereaved/)

For those of you who make resolutions, resolve to be kind to those, including yourselves, who are grieving the loss of someone or something very special.

> *"Should old acquaintance be forgot*
> *And never brought to mind?*
> *Should old acquaintances be forgot*
> *And auld lang syne (for old times' sake)"*
> ("Auld Lang Syne," Robert Burns, 1759-1796)

No. They should always be remembered and celebrated. I leave you, not with the traditional "Happy" New Year but rather wishing you a Grateful, Graceful, Hopeful and Peaceful one.

Larry's Lament

The story of an unsuccessful suicide attempt

L arry was tired. Tired of living. He was 55 years old, and his successful 33-year-old business was going downhill. There were problems at home and alcohol wasn't the solution anymore. But Larry had a plan – a plan to end his life.

He researched all the effective methods that would prove fatal. He dismissed many, as some people had survived jumping off a bridge or an overdose of pills. He discovered that the most effective method was a gun. Not to the head as we see on television, but a gun poised into his mouth. Yes, this would work.

Now he had to determine when was the best time. He didn't want to cause undue trauma by dying near his daughters' or grandchildren's birthdays, not near the holidays – it was a difficult decision. There was never a good time. He finally chose a random day and a secluded location.

He took a 12-gauge shotgun and drove out to a remote area where no one could interrupt his plan, least of all first responders. He was wrong.

His cell phone rang, and to avoid any suspicion, he answered the call. It was his sister and soulmate, Rachel. As they spoke, Rachel intuited that something was awry. She was aware of Larry's depression and she often worried about him. She didn't like the way he sounded.

Larry was trying to get her off the phone while Rachel was trying to determine his location, although she knew his solitary haunts. Rachel kept begging, "Larry, please tell me where you are!" And Larry kept repeating a single, pleading response, "Rachel, please don't do this to me."

At that moment in time, there was a beep signaling an incoming call for Larry. "Rachel, I have to take this call, it's my daughter." He cut off Rachel and switched the phone connection over to the incoming call from his daughter, Sasha. As he attempted to conduct a banal conversation with Sasha, he saw lights in the distance. *Damn,* he thought. The police and first responders were able to determine his location by "pinging" his phone.

He picked up the shotgun – a cumbersome weapon over three feet long and attempted to poise it in his mouth before the responders reached him. He had tossed his cell phone on the floor of his vehicle and thought he had pressed "end." He hadn't. Sasha was still on the phone and heard the gunshot.

In his haste, Larry put the gun in his mouth and pulled the trigger, blowing off one side of his face. He survived.

Complete mayhem ensued as they rushed Larry to the hospital. Larry was in a medically induced coma for a week and had multiple surgeries to reconstruct his face. He lost all his teeth. Rachel provided a photograph of Larry to the ENT surgeon in the hopes that the surgeon might make Larry look like himself again.

When Larry was taken out of the coma, he was angry. In fact, he was furious. He had failed. His final failure. He couldn't even be successful, even after all his meticulous planning. He had failed at death.

Everyone told him, "You're not ready yet, you still have something to accomplish. It's not your time." There were years of rehab and recovery, behavioral health groups with others who had survived suicide.

That was almost nine years ago.

Years later, Larry moved in with his dad, who needed him, and Larry care of him until his father's death. He fished, he grew his hair out and donated it to cancer patients, and he reunited with his daughters. He became a humanitarian of sorts.

I spoke to Larry this week, asking for a message for our readers. The following is his response:

"I'm a work in progress, but I've come a long way. I have more than six years sobriety. If I could relive that day, I would have demanded help. I did call both my therapist and psychiatrist as I was driving to my suicide destination, but I received voicemails, and left pleading messages.

"If any of your readers want to know if a loved one is contemplating suicide, ask them. Say the word. Suicide. Ask the question: 'Are you thinking about suicide?' The best way to stop it is to ask.

"Love them and get them help. Don't blame yourselves. There's nothing you could have done. Depression can be as fatal as cancer. We must overcome the stigma associated with suicide. I feel like I wear a scarlet letter. My suicide attempt cannot be ignored or hidden. It's not a secret I keep. I wear it every day on my face. I can't forget, and people cannot ignore."

Signs, Signs, Everywhere a Sign

It was Mother's Day. Nancy, her husband Anthony, and their two teenage sons prepared to attend a Mother's Day brunch at a local restaurant. Always a close family, Nancy was a bit disappointed as their tradition of cards, flowers, and breakfast in bed had been dismissed this year for an unexplained reason. The boys seemed less than happy as they sat in the backseat of the car, grumbling under their breaths. They would rather be playing baseball. In addition, Anthony seemed less than enthusiastic and hadn't even given her a card.

The brunch turned out to be less than celebratory for all. The restaurant was crowded and noisy, the buffet lines long and slow. The scrambled eggs were cold, and the bacon overcooked. Nancy felt that her family's efforts were obligatory at best. They ate in silence: the tension at their table was palpable, a blatant contradiction to the laughing, kissing, and hugging at the tables around them. Nancy was sad. They paid the bill, left, and drove home in uncomfortable silence. Upon arriving home, the boys grabbed their baseball gear and headed out the field. Nancy sat on the couch in angered silence.

"What's going on with you?" Anthony asked.

"Nothing."

"I know you're upset, Nancy."

Anthony continued to ask, and Nancy continually repeated "nothing." With each "nothing" her voice escalated until she was shouting. "NOTHING!" LEAVE ME ALONE." So, he did. Anthony went upstairs to take a nap. Nancy remained sitting on the couch, sobbing. It's always easier to be angry than hurt. Anger is a defense, hurt makes us vulnerable. Nancy chose anger. It fit well.

The remainder of the day passed in silence. The boys returned from the baseball field to complete their homework.

"Mom, what's for dinner? We are starving."

Nancy responded through gritted teeth, "I'm not cooking. It's Mother's Day. Order a pizza and use your allowance money to pay the delivery boy." The boys huffed and went into the kitchen. Anthony came downstairs to watch television and when the pizza arrived, he joined the boys. Nancy stayed quietly on the couch, and for the first time in their 20-year marriage, they slept apart, Nancy on the couch and Anthony upstairs in their bedroom.

Morning came slowly for Nancy. She made coffee for herself and threw in some laundry. The boys had already left for school and Anthony had left early, as his job took him out of state. When Nancy heard the ring of her cell phone, she checked and saw it was Anthony. She assumed he was calling to apologize but she wasn't going to give in that easily. Moments later her cell phone rang. It was Anthony again. She answered, rolling her eyes in the expectation of a weak 'sorry.' Or maybe, she mused, it was a "pocket dial." The connection was poor, and she couldn't understand what he was saying. She thought she heard him say "I love you" through the static.

"Anthony, I can't hear you. Call me back when you have better service."

He never called back.

The next call came from one of Anthony's colleagues. Anthony was gone, dead from a heart attack with his cell phone still in hand. Nancy fell to the floor, knowing that he had been calling her to say goodbye.

Her last words to him haunted her for years. "Call me back when you have better service."

Nancy came to me fraught with guilt, shame, and remorse. She wanted to turn back the hands of time.

"Death ends a life, not a relationship, Nancy. Look for signs."

So, she did. Every week she came to our session with examples: a license plate that she noticed at a stop sign that included Anthony's initials, his favorite song on the radio, a red cardinal in her yard. But she wasn't convinced and chalked everything up to coincidence.

She decided she might feel better if she created a legacy, and with that drove to tree farms around New England in search of a rare tree from Anthony's country of origin. It wasn't easy, but she was determined. She envisioned a park-like area in her yard with the tree as the focal point.

Each stop proved to be a disappointment, but after months of searching she found a small, unassuming tree farm that had the tree! Just one, but that was all she wanted. Just one.

She approached the owner and pointed out the tree for which she had been searching, diligently, unsuccessfully. The manager took her over to the tree.

"That's exactly what I want!" Nancy exclaimed. "I don't care about the cost."

The manager walked around the tree and showed Nancy a manila card wrapped with twine around one of the branches.

"This tree has been on hold since July; however, the gentleman never returned and didn't leave any contact information. I guess I can sell it to you."

The manager pulled the tag off the tree and handed it to Nancy.

"Please hold this while I wrap the tree for you."

Nancy held the tag and as she turned it over, she thought her heart stopped. It read:

"Hold for Anthony."

$\mathcal{B}$efore and $\mathcal{A}$fter a $\mathcal{L}$oss to Opioid Overdose

A midst the fear of the coronavirus and the media coverage of the Democratic primaries, we often forget the ongoing issues, particularly the opioid crisis. People are still overdosing. People are still dying. Please take a moment to hear a mother's plea. One mother who echoes the pain of thousands after losing a child to an unintended overdose. Ironically, this mom, Deborah Manzo McDonald is also the Director of Teen Challenge Rhode Island, a long-term inpatient recovery facility for women of all ages.

"Have you ever missed someone so much that you can't breathe? Have you ever missed someone so much that when your feet hit the floor in the morning, the crushing thought of another day brings you to your knees as they buckle under the weight of the unhealed scars on your broken heart? Have you then realized that tomorrow is today, and the rawness of the loss hasn't healed? It doesn't get easier; in fact, as time continues to pass, it assures you that your loved one is really gone. Forever.

"I sometimes force myself to echo and repeat, my son JoJo is not here anymore and he is never coming back. JoJo is not here anymore, and he is never coming back. As I say this it still doesn't sound real. Or right. How did this happen? Have you ever asked yourself, 'Why me? Why my child? When there are thousands in successful recovery?' I have. As have many others who have lost a child to an accidental drug overdose.

"Do you remember your 'before'? How does it compare to your 'after'? My before included being a mom to three boys and dedicated to my work at Teen Challenge Rhode Island. I thought I had worked tirelessly to help these girls overcome their addictions. I thought I had given my all. Until my 'after.' My after began on September 14, 2016, the day my oldest son, JoJo, died of an accidental overdose. I immediately began to hold onto the loss. I felt like a victim. How could this happen to me? It's not fair. I spent endless evenings poring over photograph albums, crying, oftentimes hysterical. I couldn't even walk through the doors of Teen Challenge. How can I work tirelessly to save addicts when my own son is dead? From the same disease! It seemed impossible. Insurmountable. At our first annual fundraiser, held shortly after JoJo's death, I sat in the car in the parking lot. I watched people of all ages and ethnicities, happy to celebrate their daughter's path to recovery. I struggled to open the car door. I closed it. I couldn't move. Grief paralyzed me. Eventually I opened the car door and got out. The walk from the car to the venue was exhausting. *How am I going to do this?* I thought. *How can I walk into this venue in front of hundreds of people celebrating the recovery journey of their loved ones? Why isn't JoJo by my side? He loved the girls at Teen Challenge.*

"I cried the entire banquet. I returned home to my photo albums, my dog, and my bed. My after will be spent this way for the rest of my life. Then God spoke to me: *You are not a victim. You will not hold onto loss. You are a survivor and will hold onto love.* It was then that I took a shower, dressed, and walked back through the doors of Teen Challenge to continue where I had left off. How could I ever disregard Paula, who in her early 20's with two children has been prostituted, beaten, raped and is now thriving at TCRI. And what about Barbara? Trafficked, abused, shot up with heroin at age five by her own father? Barbara, who stays at TCRI, feeling safe and secure? How can I turn my back on all these girls? As a victim who holds onto loss? No. As a survivor who holds onto love! It was with love that I returned with a vengeance. My 'after' is solely dedicated to the lives of these girls and to the legacy of my son. The two have merged: The JoJo McDonald 5K brings the girls, JoJo, and the community together as one.

"I know there are a great deal of you out there who may be stuck and mired in the victimhood of loss. I implore you to join us. My 'after' will always be an 'us,' never an 'I.' We cannot give up on these girls. I've seen so much success and believe that as my passion and efforts increase, so will the success of recovering addicts. Many of you, like me, have a 'before' and 'after.' Hopefully many of you have just a 'before,' but live in fear of the potential of an 'after.'

"We are an organization that exists only through donations. Our newest effort is the Women and Children's Home, so that we can take the children of our girls out of DCYF custody, out of institutions, out of foster homes, and begin to heal and mend a relationship damaged and broken because of opioids.

But we need you. Yes, YOU! Please help us continue my 'after' – through participation and/or donations. Join the 5K and celebrate your survival, your love.

"It seems like a moment ago it was the birth of the 1st Annual Joseph P. McDonald, Esq. 5K but here we are preparing for the third EPIC (it's EPIC to anyone who knew JoJo or who has come alongside the McDonald family and friends) 5K event.

"As I reflect on the first year, it was mostly about JoJo and preserving his memory, the hurt too deep for hearts to open to anything else. As I began to walk this new life without JoJo, I became aware of so many hurting people like myself. God stepped up my ministry. I now feel compelled to reach out to the ones who also experienced a loss – a son, daughter, husband, wife, sister, brother, mother, father, other family member, friend, acquaintance. People all ravaged by the opioid drug epidemic.

"In our second year, the 5K borders expanded and with that, the question to the hurting became, 'Would you like to put a sign with a picture in honor of your loved one along the 5K route this year?' On the day of the 5K there they were, all along the race route. Signs were also created of the TCRI women. 'before and after,' except the 'after' were these precious ladies rooting the participants on.

"Just writing this, even after three years, still brings so much emotion to me. Healing to the brokenhearted. A wave of love extended. Families creating teams – they make t-shirts with pictures of their loved one, they name it after that person. From what I have witnessed, this event has become a major support system for them.

"And so, I ask if you would be so kind to start a team, join a team, just run/walk, donate to this worthy cause, and pray.

"All proceeds from this race will go to fund the construction of our Women's and Children's home, a much-needed place, where the TCRI women can recover with their children being by their side in recovery as well. Out of foster care and the DCYF system and with their moms.

"This 5K is not just a fundraiser, it's an homage to my son. It helps me move forward as I acknowledge his life, our lives together, with an empty chair at the table. I invite, encourage, and welcome all of you to join me both in my pain and my healing. Come and celebrate the loss of your loved one, and let's heal together.

"As a survivor, I dedicate my life to God, my family, and Teen Challenge daily in the fight to end addiction. It is a war to be committed to in memory of our loved ones. Help carry the torch of Teen Challenge Rhode Island as we fight this epidemic every day and promote hope and healing through the unconditional love of God. We can channel our grief by fighting with determination, not just at the 5K, but every day. Let's allow this passion and commonality to bind us together. There is so much strength in numbers.

"Praise God, it is no longer impossible to breathe, but possible to shout out our pain in courage and recognize that all our tomorrows will become todays. Together, with the help of God through Teen Challenge Rhode Island, let's make today count for loved ones who are struggling before it's too late.

"Together we can LOVE them back to life."

www.josephpmcdonald5k.com

Empty Nests

"After all these years, all the smiles and the tears
I am on the other side, watching my kids take the ride
Like me they'll be too stubborn I know that they won't see
But all it is I want, for them is to be free
Happiness and heartbreak, there will be no compromise
Too young for them to focus, cannot see through those eyes"
("Through Those Eyes," Joe Martira, 2020)

The house is empty now. Gone is the ruckus and chaos of kids coming in and out of the kitchen door with a bounty of friends looking for something to eat. Gone are the days of snowstorms and cancelled school, where the bounty of my kids' friends repeated their tradition of sleeping at my house. Gone are those morning-after-the-snow breakfasts of egg, ham, and cheese on a bagel for 12. Gone are the late evenings, well past curfew, where I sit in the front window, waiting with bated breath, worried, hoping they return safely so I can simply be angry. Gone are the familiar days of my life.

I looked forward to this day. To the peace and quiet. The independence and free time. No homework, no bus schedules, no more teenage angst. It's time to empty the nest. Although I've read many articles on the loss associated with children leaving, I felt I didn't fit into that category. In fact, I chuckled. This is the beginning of the rest of my perfect, manageable, life.

And then it wasn't.

My chuckle quickly mutated into a sigh and then lonely tears. My naivete had me celebrating my children's migration from high school graduate to college bound a success story.

This quiet fostered hours of thinking about the past. The pediatrician visits, the snowsuits that were impossible to put on, youth sports, the initial nervous, vigilant days to the beach. August school shopping for new notebooks, backpacks, books, and pens, middle school dances, crushes that crushed the tender adolescent heart, high school proms, and college acceptance letters. These are still the days of my life.

Next is the flurry of preparation, tasks performed with surface enthusiasm in an attempt to delay the inevitable. Last-minute shopping trips for bedding, USB cables, and (I insisted) a pepper spray gun. Taking that long ride with an overstuffed car to campus. Helping, holding, moving, until goodbye.

I return home in an empty car, feeling both light and heavy. People say this is the next chapter. For each and all of us. I now have time to do whatever I please and whenever I please; however, I begin to grieve the loss of the lack of daily rituals and organization, the life measured by the time on the clock. I have lengthy conversations with Alexa, blast music to fill the silence, binge Netflix. And worry. And wait for what we had agreed upon – a daily call or text.

I felt I had to sound happy and reassured when I heard from them. I remember having a freshman student, Allison, from California, who was just beyond thrilled to be in New England to experience her first snowfall. One day she came into class and stated that she needed to transfer to a school back home. I spoke with her about the difficulties in being lonesome, making new friends, and managing her time.

It turns out the student was exceptionally happy at school, but she was worried about her parents. They were having a hard time, calling several times a day, sobbing over how much they missed her and how the quiet in the house was unnerving. Allison felt guilty about leaving her parents. The roles had been reversed. Six years later, Allison completed both her bachelor's degree and master's degree, and mom and dad had become creative in her absence. Allison thought they were experiencing a midlife crisis. When she returned home for holiday break, her father greeted her on his new Harley. He had acquired a mullet, black leather jacket, tattoo, and a pierced eyebrow. The shock of seeing this transformation of her dad concerned her.

What has Mom done to cope with her only daughter leaving for college? she thought.

Mom appeared to be a feudal chieftain, gliding into the room with a flowing gown of orange and yellow, a headdress that added six inches to her height, her hair braided and now down to her waist. The house was filled with incense and statues of Buddha. Allison thought of Kafka's *Metamorphosis* – her parents hadn't transformed into huge insects, but the change was palatable.

You see, we are not the only side of this relationship equation. Our children need to believe and expect that what they left would remain the same, a sturdy, steady, and safe place that smells and tastes like childhood. It's home. And we as parents? It takes a seamless amount of time to let go. Our parental role plays an important role in our lives. We will always be parents; however, our roles will morph and change. We will become confidantes to our adult children, engage in deep existential conversations, and become overcome with pride at their college graduation. And maybe add a new role of grandparent. Yet, hindsight is 20/20, so for now we prepare ourselves for the empty nest and its potential unintended consequences.

Note: In the murk and mire that is COVID, we experience an added concern, an added worry. Fuel to the fire so to speak. Will they get sick? Will they be safe? It will take time, but we find a way to replace old habits with new opportunities. As Wordsworth expressed, "Though nothing can bring back the hour of splendor in the grass, nor glory in the flower; grieve not, but rather find strength in what remains behind."

The Emperor's New Clothes

We are living in a world fraught with a minefield of words. It's almost impossible to avoid them, but I will try, as I zigzag through the mire of nouns, verbs, and adjectives. Although I prefer to be mute today, I will rally – as I never want to be compared to the emperor who has new clothes. Some of the words I choose to use are potentially explosive, but hopefully, within the context of grief and loss they are palatable.

The world is grieving. Everyone is experiencing one or more losses, and anger seems to be the popular response. Not necessarily effective, just popular. Anger is a comfortable, usually acceptable, recognizable emotion. Anger is easy.

As a professor of clinical mental health counseling, I am acutely aware (and encourage my students to be equally so) of subtexts. Anger can be like a Potemkin village, a façade that masks the truth – the masking and hiding of the true emotion, the one that makes us feel vulnerable and afraid.

Fear, hurt, rejection, and powerlessness are all too often masked as anger, also part of loss. We are scared because our world is different, and thus we feel the need to reevaluate our self-schema and worldview. Change is equally as scary for many. The perceived erosion of the symbols of our past, the questioning of our traditional cultural norms and values, the feeling of being deprived of voicing our own truth, are all reasons for fear. We are fearful of telling the emperor he has no clothes on, fearful to criticize or react to what is happening in our world right now, because of the perceived wisdom of the masses. The masses, however, are shouting out loud and clear what they see, what they perceive as their truth. It's understandable.

The current situation may be analogous to the old children's game of Red Rover. "Red Rover, Red Rover, send you right over." As our name is called, we run as fast and as hard as we can to break the connection of hands of the opposing team. Loss, anger, and fear are running hard and fast to break the connection as well. But what if the connection is the goal? Not we. Not them. But us?

This effort may seem futile, but what we do have is our ability to express ourselves. Right now. Despite our views, we need to go beyond the anger and recognize what it is. Hear the subtext. But let us, all of us, speak our truths like the little boy who disclosed what everyone was thinking – "the emperor has no clothes."

Be the little child. Do not be afraid. But do it peacefully, mercifully, respectfully and with grace. There is room for all of us.

The Perfect Storm

"I read the news today, oh boy...."
(The Beatles, "A Day in the Life," 1967)

"An election incomplete. A divisive country. COVID. New Rhode Island regulations. A subjective media. Financial instability. Daylight savings time. Interrupted traditional education. A Halloween with a blue moon. A dysmorphic Thanksgiving. These are some of the issues my clients address in their sessions. Some address all. One referred to it as a "perfect storm." A popular meme trending on Facebook states, "Remember that feeling you got when the second plane hit the twin towers and you realized what was going on? You should have that same feeling again right now."

This anxiety, this fear, this overwhelming sensation of powerlessness is pervasive regardless of one's political affiliation. I attempt to work with the potential for resilience and focus on a strengths-based approach. But first, I sit with my client's emotions, strive to hold them in my hands for a bit, alleviating their pain until they are ready to take it back.

In all cases, each of them is grieving a loss of their identity as an American. We define ourselves by our culture, our heritage, our allegiance to a country. There is comfort is knowing. Now we are questioning that role, and with it a sense of modifying that role, or perhaps relinquishing it. Do we leave that role blank, empty? Or do we replace it. But who and what is an American – now?

People are fueled with hate, vitriol, and a razor-sharp anger at what they perceive as a helplessness. So, they gather. There still is an outlet for these emotions in America. There is comfort in shared feelings and so they protest. They can still protest. For now. As one client stated, "We still have freedom. For now."

Conservatives want and offer a need for tradition and history. A wish for what was. They are fearful of a change. Not any change. This particular change. One that is being touted as a complete metamorphosis of the America they knew, know, and love. The trending alternative is just too scary.

Uber-liberals see American traditions as antiquated. They believe it's time to either abort or rebirth our country. They see our country as stuck in the past and need to change with the times.

And then there is the media, whose goal is to provide us with one side of the information and in many cases have convinced us. And therein lies the rub.

COVID proves to be a major variable in this perfect storm. Many report that this election conundrum would not exist without the institution of mail-in ballots, an effort to miti-gate the spread of the virus. But. It is what it is.

Conservatives believe they can make their own decisions and thus chose to vote in person, safely, with social distance, washing hands and wearing masks.

Uber-liberals take the government's edicts to heart and follow blindly. "This all could have been resolved with in-person, ID requirements. Like before." (Anonymous client)

We can't unchange what has happened. We can take efforts to recount the votes. But we can't change the voting process or the existence of COVID.

However, we do have power. We do have choices, albeit limited. We have the power and the choice as to how we respond to the storm. Take care of ourselves. Prepare our bodies for the emotional onslaught. Turn off the television. Listen to music. Take a walk. And another walk. Breathe the good air, not the divisive air that clogs our lungs, makes it difficult to breathe, elicits sharp chest and belly pains. We rant and we rave.

There are not enough therapists in America to meet the needs of the suffering in 2020 and 2021. COVID and quarantine has exponentially increased our hunger for freedom and choice. "The strict governors have shut off our air supply with their unneeded rules." "Why does our governor punish everyone in the state for the behavior of the few." (client). "Doesn't she know anything about reward and punishment to change behavior? What she is doing won't work. She will get pushback from those of us who have been "behaving" correctly." (client- "behavior" in quotes as it was said sarcastically).

No doubt, whatever the course of the virus and the result of the election, depression, anxiety, substance abuse, and suicide will all increase, as well as family cohesion and the erosion of quality education and the economy. "The cure should not be worse than the cause (virus)." "Fear mongering by politicians is working." (client). People voted for or against a person, not for an ideology or philosophy. I've heard some of my suburban mom friends say, "I'm voting for Biden - he is so good-looking." (client.) "I'm moving to New Zealand." (client). "I'm moving to Iceland." (client) But to what end?

There is some consolation. The conservatives still hold the Senate. The liberals still hold the House. Whatever the result of the election, we still have a democracy. We will all be represented.

I wish you all peace of mind and soul. I know that is what I strive for. I have to remain strong and intact and to genuinely hold your hurt and pain in the palm of my hand and in my heart during this perfect storm.

Snowstorm Reveries

"Though nothing can bring back the hour
Of splendor in the grass,
of glory in the flower,
We will grieve not, rather find
Strength in what remains behind."
(William Wordsworth, from his poem
"Ode: Intimations of Immortality," 1804)

In this quote, Wordsworth encourages us to find splendor and excitement in everyday, mundane situations and objects, as we did when we saw the world through younger eyes. Today, I woke to the splendor of snow, which to me has a cleansing, almost spiritual effect. For a short while, the world is still and so is my mind. Thoughts creep through, not at their usual lightning speed as brief frenetic thoughts, but rather in snippets of nostalgic memories. These same memories might cause me pause or heartache at another time, but the snow settles them and provides a precious space and time to recollect and reflect.

I sit here next to the Christmas tree, lights ablaze in the daylight. A particularly special ornament, elegant in its simplicity sits on a prominent branch. A hand-blown translucent ball covered with snow. One of the many unique gifts she gave me.

A hand painted white piano key holds my place in the book I am currently reading. Another gift, another reminder.

Snow keeps falling without a sound as I think of Gail. (Not surprising as this storm is named after her.) Thinking of her brings a sense of serenity. She was never a storm, but a beacon in the darkness. A woman who was humble, wise, and never shared her pain. She just lived with it until she couldn't.

I was walking my newborn son. He was a few months old and as I slowly pushed the stroller through the neighborhood, I noticed a new neighbor sitting on the front steps of a house that had just been built. She was pregnant. Like many relationships, it started with a quick introduction and in subsequent days, lengthy conversations. Her son was born soon after. It didn't seem serendipitous at the time. Just the way life was supposed to be.

Of course, our sons grew up together and were the best of friends. And still are, thirty-two years later. Gail would take the annual photograph of the two of them at the bus stop, from kindergarten on. If I flip through them quickly, it becomes a movie of their aging. Taller. Older. Perhaps wiser, as in the early pictures their lives are untouched by pain and grief.

I watch the snow fall and think of the boys' confirmation. Gail had saved me a seat in the church but couldn't kneel when prodded. She was experiencing strong pains in her back – she whispered that it seemed to be a tennis injury (Gail was a competitive tennis player). The MRI showed a different kind of

injury. Multiple Myeloma. Gail lived a full life, always, even after the diagnosis. A stem cell transplant granted her a few additional years and she traveled abroad with her husband and children. She was the unjudging ear I sought out throughout my life.
We swapped out our favorite books, created a two-person book
club, and she never complained. Today I think of Gail not with
grief and sadness but with a comforting solace. Her son spends
many holidays with us. Still.

My mind slows down, and a new image appears. It is
filled with adolescent boys, celebrating school cancellations due
to the snow. It was a tradition. As soon as they boys heard "no
school," their parents would drop them off at my house before
the first flake fell. Sometimes six of them, sometimes twelve. The
noise increased exponentially with their laughter and teasing.
They would each find a place to sleep for the night. A nook
somewhere in the house. In the morning I woke to unidentifiable
humps of blankets on the floor, on the couches, in chairs. Once I
found one sleeping on top of my washer/dryer!

Next came the flurry of mismatched ski jackets and
pants, hats, gloves, and boots. Many had been resurrected from
the last snowstorm, or the previous year. They spent hours
building igloos, as my mom before me had taught us to do, pouring water over the finished "fort" to solidify its permanence. I
still have some of those random hats and gloves in my closet.

Hours later, a mass of soaking wet, flushed-cheeked boys
trampled back into my house for hot chocolate and bagel sandwiches. Gail would always call to check in on her son with her
usual query, "How is everything going at Camp Mari?!"

Perhaps thinking of Gail brought my mind to those
"Camp Mari" days. I took them all to Boston one year for the

Patriots celebratory parade. The Pats had won the Super Bowl. We would always go to the infamous "Cheers" for lunch and enter the competition for consumption of the "Normburger." The prize was their picture on the wall. Some are probably still there. We would then trample through FAO Schwartz as the boys ran up and down the escalator and sat in the laps of the biggest stuffed bear, a photo shoot opportunity that still lives on in both my mind and in my photo album. The day always ended with a train ride home, each boy asleep full of joy, celebration, burgers, and magic. And the inevitable call from Gail – "How was the field trip with Camp Mari?!"

In other winters I would take them for a weekend up to the New Hampshire house. It was customary to watch Stephen King's *The Stand* late at night and go sledding and then swimming in the association's indoor pool the following day. They had their favorite restaurants in Waterville as well. And of course, the check-in call from Gail – "How are the boys doing at Camp Mari North?!"

The snow has made me peacefully pensive. There are no interruptions. No texts, no calls, no television. Just me sitting by the tree, looking at the ornaments and the snow falling. I haven't breathed this deeply and slowly in a long time. Nature has put life on pause, albeit for just a short while. I have a long to-do list sitting in my office. I don't feel pressured. I seize this opportunity to find splendor in the snow, and glory in the memories of snow and Gail so long ago.

Merry Christmas, Gail. I think of you often. With love.

Borrow Mine

If there comes a day you can't find your smile, borrow mine
If there comes a day you can't find the strength, borrow mine
If there comes a day you can't find your voice, borrow mine

Borrow whatever you need to help you get through
To help you do what you need to do
For as long as you need or until you are fine
Borrow mine

For the days you can't see what you mean to me, look to me
For the days you can't feel what you mean to me, reach for me
For the days you can't hear what you mean to me, listen to me

Please, borrow whatever you need to help you get through
To help you do what you need to do
For as long as you need or until you are fine

(Lyrics reprinted with permission. Joe Matira, March 2021.)

About the Author

In addition to being a "Mortician's Daughter," Dr. Mari Dias is a nationally board-certified counselor, holds a Fellow in Thanatology and is certified in both grief counseling and complicated grief. She also holds certificates as a Death Doula and in Psychological Autopsy Training.

She is Professor of Clinical Mental Health, Master of Science program, Johnson & Wales University. Dias is the director of GracePoint Grief Center in North Kingstown, Rhode Island. For more information, go to http://gracepointegrief.com/

Made in the USA
Columbia, SC
14 April 2021